GW00650154

ᴄ✿DIVINATION✿ᴐ

Inspiring | Educating | Creating | Entertaining

Brimming with creative inspiration, how-to projects, and useful
information to enrich your everyday life, Quarto Knows is a favorite
destination for those pursuing their interests and passions. Visit our
site and dig deeper with our books into your area of interest:
Quarto Creates, Quarto Cooks, Quarto Homes, Quarto Lives,
Quarto Drives, Quarto Explores, Quarto Gifts, or Quarto Kids.

First published in 2021 by Wellfleet Press,
an imprint of The Quarto Group,
142 West 36th Street, 4th Floor,
New York, NY 10018, USA
T (212) 779-4972 F (212) 779-6058
www.QuartoKnows.com

Wellfleet titles are also available at discount for retail, wholesale, promotional, and bulk purchase. For details,
contact the Special Sales Manager by email at specialsales@quarto.com or by mail at The Quarto Group, Attn:
Special Sales Manager, 100 Cummings Center Suite, 265D, Beverly, MA 01915 USA.

10 9 8 7 6 5 4 3 2 1

Library of Congress Control Number: 2021939953

ISBN: 978-1-57715-261-3

Publisher: Rage Kindelsperger
Creative Director: Laura Drew
Managing Editor: Cara Donaldson
Cover and Interior Design: Ashley Prine/Tandem Books

Printed in China

This book provides general information on various widely known and widely accepted practices that tend to
evoke feelings of strength and confidence. However, it should not be relied upon as recommending or promoting
any specific diagnosis or method of treatment for a particular condition, and it is not intended as a substitute for
medical advice or for direct diagnosis and treatment of a medical condition by a qualified physician. Readers who
have questions about a particular condition, possible treatments for that condition, or possible reactions from the
condition or its treatment should consult a physician or other qualified healthcare professional.

The Quarto Group denounces any and all forms of hate, discrimination, and oppression and does not condone the
use of its products in any practices aimed at harming or demeaning any group or individual.

IN FOCUS

DIVINATION

Your Personal Guide

STEVEN BRIGHT

WELLFLEET
PRESS

CONTENTS

INTRODUCTION

Divination is the practice of extracting hidden information and meaning using what could be described as supernatural means. A diviner or reader (both terms used for someone who performs divination) will predict or look into the future, as well as present situations and sometimes even the past, using a tool or other external source as an oracle—a means of guidance. Seemingly random signs or symbols will become organized through their interpretation in a way that will provide insight, inspiration, and direction.

The art of divination is far from new. It has been around as long as human beings have existed. People have always desired to know what will happen next, and devising systems to find out what fate has in store for them and those around them goes back as far as that desire. Our needs, and in turn the subjects of our inquiries, might be different from those of our early ancestors, but many of us are still intrigued by an unknown future and curious about the ways in which we might be able to improve it.

Some ancient forms of divination may seem primitive to us now, but despite the evolution of oracles and divinatory tools, some methods have remained popular throughout history or gone by the wayside only to regain popularity. While observing the entrails of animals (practiced by shamans in antiquity) is thankfully not a favored form of divination today, diviners still use many methods that draw on our natural environment and make use of the world around us, such as floromancy (divination through flowers) and conchomancy (divination using seashells).

In this book, we will look into some of the ways in which we can practice divination. This will range from the most popular, such as reading cards and runes, to the lesser known, like color reading and even using buttons as oracles. Each chapter will engage with a different practice, suggesting ways in which a new diviner can experiment with different forms of each method.

How to Use this Book

This book provides an overview of many kinds of divination, focusing on some of the most well-known forms, but I have also handpicked a few less obvious varieties to enhance your knowledge and inspire your curiosity. You can go through them from start to finish, or you may wish to jump around

between the chapters that catch your eye. Within each section, you will find ways of using certain tools as well as common systems of interpretation. There is certainly more than enough information provided to get the new diviner started, and if one or more method sparks your interest, there are plenty of more in-depth resources out there. Once you have absorbed the basics, it really is up to you put your own stamp on each method through practice and further exploration.

Some methods require you to purchase a few items if you want to try them out, such as particular oracle decks or crystals. I provide suggestions on how you can purchase those items affordably, but for the most part, I have suggested ways in which tools can be created at home. There is something in this book for everyone, and diviners are encouraged to make use of what they already have on hand for magical purposes.

What Else Do You Need to Know?

Divination can be fun and illuminating, but it is also important that we remember to be responsible. A reading gives a snapshot of a situation and an idea of how it *could* develop, but we must be mindful of our own free will and that of those we read for. One of the beautiful parts of reading an oracle is that we can make changes in our lives on the basis of the information we receive, so if we don't like the way something is predicted to turn out, a few different choices or tweaks in the present could avoid an undesirable future.

As you embark on your own magical journey, people around you will naturally become curious and want you to do readings for them. This can be a lot of fun, but remember that some people are more sensitive than others. The oracle is a device for helping people find the best possible way of navigating through life or of dealing with a specific problem. While it is important to pass on the messages you receive, a good reader will find a method of presenting the information to the querent or questioner (interchangeable terms for the person who is receiving a reading) in a way that is tactful, compassionate, and empowering.

How to Prepare for a Reading

While many methods of divination are covered in this book, the way in which a reader approaches all these different tools can be quite similar. The following tips will enhance any reading, regardless of whether you are using cards, small objects, or tea leaves.

Set aside time when you know you will not be disturbed. There is nothing worse than beginning a reading, only to be distracted by a phone call, a hungry pet, family, or housemates. Some people set aside a specific time of day they know will be quieter. It's best if you have an hour free to really concentrate on what you are doing without interruptions.

Make sure that you have a surface that is clean and has enough room to lay out your chosen tool of divination. If you are using cards, make sure that the space is large enough to conduct your reading. If you are casting stones or charms, as an example, consider ways to keep them from falling to the ground and becoming lost. Some diviners use a tray to cast on for this reason.

A glass of water or a cup of tea, kept at a safe distance, is often a good idea as readings can be thirsty work. A drink can also add pauses to your reading, which give you time to reflect on the information you are receiving.

Some diviners like to say an affirmation or short prayer prior to reading. They might say something like, "Thank you for the information and wisdom I am about to acquire. I will endeavor to receive this information with an open mind, and I intend to use what I learn responsibly."

Take some time to consider what you would like to know and form a question around it. A question can concern any subject, though many readers prefer to not read about health, leaving such inquiries to the professionals. A good question will receive a clear answer. For instance, broad questions that emphasize what you can do to make a better future will garner better responses than asking direct questions like, "Will I get promoted?" You might be better off asking something like, "What can I do to help myself get a promotion?"

While you do not have to decorate your reading space before a session, doing so can be an effective way of preparing yourself, physically and emotionally, for a reading. A few favorite objects, such as crystal spheres, figurines, or images of an ancestor or deity, can help you become calm and focused.

Ritual can also be useful in divination. While trying new things can be refreshing and aid your practice, having a set way of doing things can help keep your practice ordered and reminds you that what you are doing is sacred. Some diviners like to wash their hands before a reading, light some incense, or play a relaxing piece of music to set the scene and get them in the required mood. This is individual to each reader.

Once you have finished your reading, putting your tools away safely is important. This will keep things from becoming broken or lost, but it also shows respect for what you are doing. A small prayer of thanks to spirit guides, if you use them, or even to the tool itself is a way of closing down the session. You might want to go for a short walk afterward to shake away the energies of your reading.

Enclosed Divination Wall Chart

Included in this book is a wall chart that serves as a quick and handy reference guide to a few types of divination that are explored on the following pages.

❋ ❋ ❋

1

LENORMAND CARDS

Card reading, also known as "cartomancy," is probably the best-known form of divination, and it has been practiced throughout the world for centuries. Using decks of cards is a popular way to divine, giving the user a portable system that they can use on the go, should they wish. Tarot is by far the most popular cartomancy system, and there is a lot of easily accessible information available on it, so I decided to talk about some other less well-known decks.

Over the last ten years, the Lenormand cards have increased in popularity. Readers, already familiar with the tarot's delicate and mysterious whispers, have become intrigued by this deck, but they are also sometimes astounded by the harsh, younger voice of the Lenormand. Whereas the tarot cards can tap into our subconscious, uncovering our hopes and fears, the Lenormand's ability to tell it how it is can be refreshingly accurate for many.

It is worth noting the differences between the Lenormand cards and the tarot since these will highlight why each has its own place within the world of divination. Unlike the tarot, the Lenormand is not divided into suits. In fact, every card has the same value. There are no major or minor sections, and the numbers assigned to each card have no numerological significance. The people incorporated into the cards are not set apart from the remainder of the deck, as found in the tarot.

One of the biggest differences between the tarot and the Lenormand, however, is that each card of the latter contains one primary symbol to be interpreted. For example, a reader can decide to focus on any number of different aspects incorporated into a tarot card (such as its general mood, colors, or a handful of occult references added to the design), whereas any extra detailing or surrounding imagery is irrelevant in the Lenormand. For example, only the central animal in the Dog card is of any significance. This is why the Lenormand usually looks sparser than the tarot, and that is potentially what makes them sharper.

The Lenormand is a relatively new system, developed around the latter part of the eighteenth century. The oldest decks in existence can be found in the British Museum in London, and they date back to 1799. The name comes from a legendary card reader, Marie Anne Lenormand, who is said to have worked in the salons of Paris with a deck that is the basis of what we see today. Probably the most famous card reader in the world, then and now, it is said that she gave predictions to Napoleon and Josephine Bonaparte. The original name of this deck, however, was The Game of Hope, and its connection to Madame Lenormand came about after her death. This means it was most likely named after her for publicity and marketing purposes.

Structure and Symbols

There are thirty-six cards in a standard Lenormand pack. They start with Clover (a card associated with luck) and end with Stork (which brings about change). Within the cards, you will find two people—the Man and Woman— either of which can signify the person being read for. If the questioner is male, then Man will signify him, and Woman will represent the person closest to him of the opposite sex. Over time, the deck has evolved to become more diverse, with some packs adding extra "people" cards for those asking about same-sex relationships. Racial diversity has also become a welcome addition.

Since the Lenormand seems to be derived from playing cards, many packs include a small playing card inset in the corner of the cards and use the associated numbers and symbols discreetly in the design. For instance, the 10 of spades is related to Ship and the 7 of hearts is linked to Tree. The face cards from regular playing card decks (jack, queen, and king) are included too, and they give us a handful of references to personality traits that can be used within a reading, should the reader wish. For instance, the king of spades, found on Lily (a card connected to maturity), can relate to an older, wise male.

Learning the Lenormand Cards

It is important to note that there is more than one school of Lenormand thought; the most common are the French and German methods. While the definitions of each card remain mostly the same across systems, there are some variations. For instance, in the French system, the Lily is a symbol for old age and wisdom and the Whip is reserved for matters of a sexual nature, whereas in the German tradition the Lily signifies sexual attraction. The meanings that follow derive from the French method.

1 Rider/ 9 of Hearts

News, new beginnings, a visitor, action, athletic, a possible love interest

2 Clover/ 6 of Diamonds

Luck, small fortune, a win, a fortunate opportunity, surprises

3 Ship/ 10 of Spades

Movement, travel, vacation, foreign shores, international travel, physical journeys

4 House/ King of Hearts

The home, security, family matters, comfort, safety

The king of hearts might represent a warm father figure.

5 Tree/7 of Hearts

Health, the physical body, well-being, roots, ancestors, growth

6 Clouds/ King of Clubs

Confusion, depression, problems, uncertainty, instability, difficulties

The king of clubs can represent a gloomy and pessimistic individual. Note: Clouds are usually depicted with a dark and light side. If a card sits on the side of the cloud that is darker, it is often influenced by the negative connotations of Clouds.

7 Snake/ Queen of Clubs

A warning, seduction, troubles ahead, deceitful, an attack, lies or gossip

The queen of clubs can sometimes represent someone to be cautious of.

8 Coffin/ 9 of Diamonds

Endings, finality, difficult changes, long illness, defeat

9 Bouquet/ Queen of Spades

Joy, gifts, compliments, beautiful things, positivity, happiness

The queen of spades represents an attractive woman with a pleasant demeanor.

10 Scythe/ Jack of Diamonds

Cutting away, abrupt damage, shock, violence, a swift act

The jack of diamonds is assertive and straightforward, sometimes tactless, and harsh.

11 Whip/ Jack of Clubs

Repetition, physical exertion, sex, arguments, anger

The jack of clubs might be argumentative but also a "player" who is interested in sexual conquests but not commitment.

12 Birds/ 7 of Diamonds

Conversation, verbal communication, chat, gossip, negotiation

13 Child/ Jack of Spades

Children, young adults, something small, innocence, naivety, a fresh start

The jack of spades could denote someone who is playful, inexperienced, or even childish.

14 Fox/ 9 of Clubs

Cunning, sneakiness, shiftiness, untrustworthy, a trickster, insincerity, a need to be alert, the "work" card

15 Bear/ 10 of Clubs

Strength, authority figure, intimidating, mother, motherhood, a boss

16 Stars/ 6 of Hearts

Hope, focus, wishes, inspiration, connection, technology

17 Stork/ Queen of Hearts

Change, improvement, transition, pregnancy, birth

The queen of hearts is a kind and compassionate woman who is traditionally fair and could be tall.

18 Dog/ 10 of Hearts

A friend, trustworthy, reliable, faithful partner, a dog or pet, friendship

19 Tower/
6 of Spades

Something big, security, perspective, corporations, large buildings, institutions, isolation

20 Garden/
8 of Spades

Meeting place, gathering, public area, an event, community, group activities

21 Mountain/
8 of Clubs

Obstacle, something that blocks, challenges, delays, the need to find a new way of doing something

22 Crossroads/
Queen of Diamonds

Choices, opportunities, more than one option, a decision to be made, being indecisive

The queen of diamonds might turn up in a reading as someone who can give help and bring about opportunities.

23 Mice/
7 of Clubs

Theft, loss, anxiety, stress, decay, damage, worries, pests

24 Heart/
Jack of Hearts

Love, romance, tenderness, a potential lover, passion

The jack of hearts is indicative of a lover who can be charming and attentive.

25 Ring/
Ace of Clubs

Unions, marriage, bonds, partnerships

26 Book/
10 of Diamonds

Knowledge, learning, education, secrets, something hidden

Note: the card nearest to the spine of the book in the reading is what is concealed. The card on the edge of the book that opens concerns what will be revealed.

27 Letter/
7 of Spades

Documents, written correspondence, mail, email, written invitations, and communication

28 Man/
Ace of Hearts

The male being read for or the closest or most relevant male to the querent, should the querent be female

29 Woman/ Ace of Spades

The female being read for or the closest or most relevant female to the querent, should the querent be male

30 Lily/ King of Spades

Age, wisdom, maturity, things that take a long time, passivity

The king of spades can represent a wise and mature man who is calm and in a position to give sound advice.

31 Sun/ Ace of Diamonds

Success, warmth, accomplishment, recognition, praise, optimism, joy, victory

32 Moon/ 8 of Hearts

Public image, fame, popularity, intuition, imagination

33 Key/ 8 of Diamonds

Solution, a "yes," positive outcome, access, success

34 Fish/ King of Diamonds

Money, cash flow, assets, trade, finances, abundance

The king of diamonds can represent a financier, someone who has a lot of money, or someone who can give financial advice.

35 Anchor/ 9 of Spades

Stability, dedication, endurance, steady, stubborn, persistent, not moving

36 Cross/ 6 of Clubs

Burden, difficulty, sacrifice, grief, suffering, hardship

How Is the Lenormand Read?

One of the main differences between reading the Lenormand and reading the tarot is that the Lenormand cards are not read singly. While pulling one every day for study is a good method for learning the meanings, they are most often read in pairs or groups. This allows for the meanings to become sharper, which accounts for their accuracy. Whereas a tarot card can tell a whole story in isolation, the Lenormand cards might be viewed as single words, which, when strung together, will make a coherent sentence.

If we pair two of the cards we have already spoken about, Lily (age) and Dog (friendship), we could be looking at an older person or lifelong friend. Stork (change) and Clover (luck) could mean a change of luck when read together.

Reading Pairs

The smallest reading I recommend for the Lenormand is a pairing, and there are a few ways in which this can be done. It is worth noting that different approaches may garner slightly different interpretations.

If we think about each card as being a component in a larger story, we could read them from left to right, as follows:

Lily (age, long time) + Dog (friendships, trustworthy) = It has been a long time since I last saw my good friend.

However, if we look at the first card as the main source of our message and use the second as a card of context, the pair could be read differently:

Lily (age, wisdom) + Dog (friendships, trustworthy) = wise friend.

How you choose to read your pairs is up to you, but as with all methods of divination, it will strengthen your readings if you are consistent in your approach. Knowing how you are going to interpret the positioning before you turn the cards will help with accuracy.

The Three-Card Reading

Three cards can be interpreted in the same ways as a pair. They can be read as a sentence, adding a little more to the overall message as you move from left to right:

Lily (age, wisdom) + Dog (friendships, trustworthy) + Garden (meeting place, gathering) = It has been a long time since I have seen my good friend, and we have arranged to meet.

You can also choose to read the cards with one as a main source. With this method, the middle card is often given primary focus. This means that there are actually two pairings in the reading. Let's look at the same example. As you can see, the interpretation is slightly altered:

Lily (age, wisdom) + Dog (friendships, trustworthy) + Garden (meeting place, gathering)

Dog (friendships, trustworthy) + Lily (age, wisdom) = old friend

Dog (friendships, trustworthy) + Garden (meeting place, gathering) = sociable friend

These cards will, of course, make more sense when in the context of an answer to a question. The more proficient you become at reading in this way, extra cards can be added, extending the line of cards to five or more.

The Focused Three-Card Reading

It is possible to activate a card within the deck, should you have a specific subject in mind. If, for instance, you want to know about your romantic life, then you would choose Heart card out of the deck; if it is your career you are asking about, then Fox would be the best choice. Once you have decided which card to focus on, shuffle your deck face down as you normally would and, once finished, turn the cards over and fan through them until you find the activated card. The card on either side of it can be read as context. The closer your card is to the start of your deck, the greater significance it will have.

The Box Spread

Once you have mastered the two- and three-card methods, it will be easier to interpret larger layouts. The Box Spread, when broken down, is actually a series of three-card readings, with the central card carrying extra weight. Should Book (knowledge, secrets) sit within the middle of the nine, the reading might concern education or even things you might not yet be aware of.

The cards can be read in rows and columns. Some people will assign different meanings to each, such as the left column concerning things that have happened in the past, the middle column showing the present, and the final column offering a prediction for the future. The rows may suggest different areas of life, such as home, work, and love. You are encouraged to play around with different ideas and see which best suits your needs.

The nine cards in the Box Spread can be read in a multitude of ways, and you are invited to find your own way of interpreting it. The reading can be complex. If you wish to extract a great deal of information from it, the cards can be read diagonally, or you can make use of the corner cards. The basics described here will provide a thorough and detailed reading without getting too complicated.

The Grand Tableau

The Grand Tableau uses all thirty-six cards from the deck and can be an intimidating layout for the beginner. There are different ways of laying out this spread, but the most common is in four horizontal rows of eight with a further four placed at the bottom, as shown on the next page. The Grand Tableau, which means "the big picture," is ideal for someone who wants to gain insight into a variety of areas.

Each position within the Grand Tableau is considered. From left to right, each of the positions (called houses) relate to the card's sequence within the deck: position one is related to the Rider, for example, while the Clover is

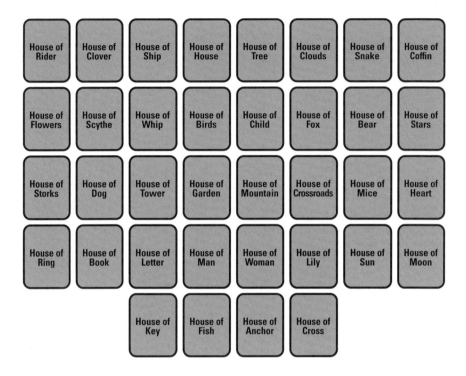

position two, and so on. Remembering the order of the cards is not easy, so many diviners have a printed cloth to lay their reading on or some kind of cheat sheet for reference.

When the cards are shuffled and laid into these positions, their natural inclination is to work together. For instance, if the Ship (movement, travel) lands on position one (Rider: news, new beginnings), you would be inclined to suspect that news will come from afar or that a vacation might be coming up. If the Whip (repetition, arguments) falls on position fourteen (Fox: cunning, the "work" card), you could deduce that work has become repetitive or that there is some kind of dispute in the workplace.

Much can be learned from the relationship between card and position, but the Grand Tableau is far more than just that. When you stand back from the reading, you will see that it encompasses many three-card readings, lines, and Box Spreads. In fact, if you wish to know about a specific area of life, you can find the card representing what you wish to know about (such as Fish for finances) and read the eight cards around it for further information. Depending on where the card has fallen, however, a Box Spread will not always be possible. If it is at the top, bottom, or sides of a reading, you cannot use the Box Spread.

Should a specific row or column be cut away, then that means the information cannot be disclosed, it may no longer be relevant to the situation, or perhaps it hasn't yet developed enough for you to read into the future about it.

Cleansing Your Cards

Many readers like to cleanse their cards either before they use them or after conducting a number of readings. This can be done in a variety of ways. Some will wave each card through incense smoke individually, while others prefer to order their deck (putting it back together in suits or ordering by number) to clear it of the energies imbued by other people or readings. Many card readers enjoy cleansing their cards by leaving them on the windowsill overnight when there is a full moon, allowing the moonlight to rid their deck of any unwanted or negative energies.

How to Bring the Magic of the Lenormand into Your Life

There are many Lenormand decks on the market, and they come in a multitude of styles, ranging from the antique to the bold and modern. When buying a set, it is important to check the dimensions of the cards since larger cards are hard to fit on a table if you wish to tackle the Grand Tableau. Cards with simpler designs are easier to read—you do not want to misidentify a card in a reading while hunting through the imagery to locate the symbol.

If you'd like to dip your toes into the Lenormand without spending any money, you can easily adapt a standard playing card deck. Since you have the corresponding playing card references here, you can simply write the names of the Lenormand cards on the playing deck (eliminating the sixteen unused cards), and even write in a few of the meanings if you like. This is an effective way to learn the system with minimal expense. If you're artistically minded, you may wish to add a little doodle or illustration of the symbol on each card.

✳ ✳ ✳

2

KIPPER CARDS

The Kipper cards are somewhat similar to the Lenormand cards. Alike in size and comprising thirty-six cards, the Kipper is also read in groups rather than singly. Unlike the Lenormand, however, the Kipper is not symbolic. Where the Lenormand uses a symbolic language, referencing an animal like fox to represent work, the Kipper is even more straightforward. Cards such as Work, Marriage, Dishonesty, and Court remove the mystery from this oracle, leaving the reader in no doubt as to what a reading is telling them.

The Kipper cards originated in Germany in the 1890s. It is said that Suzanne Kipper, whom the cards are named after, had learned both the Gypsy Cards (another oracle deck popular at the time) and Lenormand systems and was well known for her fortune-telling abilities in her hometown of Berlin. After she moved south to the German state of Bavaria, it is said that she found her audiences didn't like the Lenormand or Gypsy Cards. To better please her clients, Kipper set about creating a deck that had an everyday feel to it, without symbols that could offend those with more sensitive natures.

As with the story of Marie Anne Lenormand, we have no real evidence that the cards we read today bear any resemblance to those used by Suzanne Kipper, and including her name in the title might have been no more than a marketing ploy. The cards are situational and easier to grasp than the Lenormand, and this has led them to become increasingly popular in recent years, though they do come with their own complexities. The Kipper cards are broken up in their own way and carry directional clues for reading.

Kipper Card Meanings

Here are the common ways to interpret the cards of this deck.

Card	Meaning
1 Main Character	Male querent; otherwise, male significant other
2 Main Character	Female querent; otherwise, female significant other
3 Marriage	Partnership, bonds, connections, commitments, marriage
4 Convene	Meetings, social events, gatherings
5 Good Gent	Kindly gentleman, good news, support, positivity, leadership, older man
6 Good Lady	Kind lady, older woman, maternal, affectionate, well-meaning advice
7 Letter	Communications, paperwork, messages, updates, sealed contracts
8 Dishonesty	Deceit, trickery, untrustworthy people, false friends, betrayal
9 Change	Change of routine, lifestyle differences, movement, life shift
10 Journey	Direction, exploration, growth, transport, traveling
11 Win Lots	Material gain, abundance, new wealth, financial success, good fortune

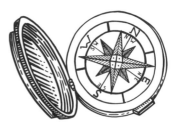

Card	Meaning
12 Rich Girl	Carefree youth, sociable, light-hearted, spirited, a best friend, vibrant
13 Rich Gent	Ambitious, idealistic, motivated, driven, colleague, competitive
14 Sad News	Sadness, grief, sudden and shocking news, disappointment
15 Good Outcome	Positive outcome, satisfaction, love, friendship, peace
16 His Thoughts	Thoughts, ideas, romance, affection, planning
17 Gift	Surprises, gift, invitation, offer, proposal, compliment
18 Infant	New beginnings, a child, playfulness, pregnancy, freshness
19 Fatality	Endings, finality, separation, death, termination
20 House	Stability, a home, structure, where you live
21 Living Room	Living area, apartment, internal, intimate, privacy
22 Military Person	An official person, someone in uniform, authority, discipline, guarded, order
23 Court	A courthouse, justice, legalities, resolution, formalities, official buildings
24 Theft	Loss, theft, deterioration, a need for caution

Card	Meaning
25 High Honors	Accomplishment, promotion, praise, recognition, institutions, reward
26 Great Fortune	Luck, well-being, positive change, spiritual growth, fate
27 Unexpected Money	Money, upturn of finances, unexpected funds, improvement
28 Expectation	Longing, aspiration, anticipation, patience, desires
29 Prison	Vast buildings, isolation, secretive, constraining situations, punishment
30 Court Official	Advice, conflict resolution, necessary processes
32 Sorrow	Stresses, busy times, confusion, anxiety, focusing on things we'd rather not
33 Gloomy Thoughts	Depression, sadness, psychological problems, negative thoughts
34 Work	Work, job, effort, labor, determination, daily activities
35 Long Way	Long distance, slow movement, great amount of time, take your time
36 Hope Great Water	Hopes, dreams, destination, overseas, goals are met, contentment

Structure

Each of the cards within the Kipper deck appears to have the same value, though this is not entirely true. In fact, there is a structure hidden within plain sight. Modern Kipper author Toni Puhle teaches that there are groupings within the thirty-six cards and being able to identify these can vastly improve readings. In the deck that Puhle and I created together, which is called the Rainbow Kipper, we color coded each of the different groups to make them easier to spot in a large reading.

The groupings are as follows.

Main Characters

The two Main Character cards signify the person questioning the cards: a male or female. The second gender is the person (of either sex) that is closest to the questioner or who is the prime focus of the reading. In the Rainbow Kipper, we include an extra male card and another female card for the benefit of those who wish to read about same-sex relationships. Only two cards should be included in the reading though (whether male and female, male and male, or female and female) and the direction they face is of importance. If they face each other in a Grand Tableau (a spread using all thirty-six cards), then a positive relationship is noted. If they sit back-to-back or are far away from each other, there may be a fractured relationship or the people may be at odds with each other.

People Cards

Good Gent, Good Lady, Rich Girl, Rich Gent, Child

These cards suggest people who may be relevant in the questioner's life.

Stop Cards

Letter, Win Lots, Good Outcome, His Thoughts, House, Living Room, Military Person, Court, High Honors, Great Fortune, Unexpected Money, Prison, Sorrow, Work, Hope Great Water

These cards punctuate lines of cards, showing us where the action or storyline finishes.

Movement Cards

Change, Journey, Gift, Long Way

These cards suggest movement and a direction for the reader to follow: they lead the story toward something.

Connector Cards

Marriage, Convene, Court Official, Short Illness

These cards bring the two cards that flank them together, connecting situations in a reading.

Cause and Effect Cards

Dishonesty, Sad News, Fatality, Theft, Expectation, Gloomy Thoughts

Surrounding cards will help to explain what is happening in these cards, given their placement. In the example shown below, the card behind the thief will show what has been taken, and the card following it will highlight how the

seeker has been affected by the theft. In the example, you can deduce that money has been taken and that the questioner will need to work hard to replace it. While there are many directional possibilities and reading techniques for the Kipper, we will start small and cover only a little of this information as a foundation for using this oracle.

A Simple Kipper Reading

Shuffle your deck of cards, remembering to decide on which Main Character you identify with. The card you choose is called your Significator. If you identify with the male character, you will read to the direction of his line of sight. If you identify as female, then you would read in the opposite direction. In traditional Kipper reading, a male-identifying person reads to the right and a female-identifying person reads to the left but the directions might be different in your deck.

Once you have mixed the cards enough, turn the deck over to face you. Go through each card until you reach your Significator. What card came before it? What card follows it? Remove these cards and look at them in a line of three. The card that sits behind the Significator could suggest an obstacle or something that the questioner is struggling to deal with, therefore requiring attention.

The card that falls ahead of your Significator is auspicious. This is something that you will be able to either do well or a problem that you will overcome. Gloomy Thoughts, ahead of the Significator, would suggest that any negative thoughts from this experience can be handled.

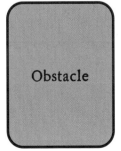
Obstacle

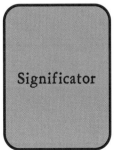
Significator

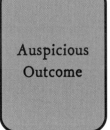
Auspicious Outcome

Larger Spreads

It is important to remember that the larger Kipper spreads are made up of many smaller ones. The beauty of the Kipper cards is that they allow for the reader to focus on different areas of action or interest, with the different groupings helping to direct our attention to what is going on. The Grand Tableau, which uses all thirty-six cards, has various pockets of information that will be of interest to the reader. (See pages 19–21 in the Lenormand chapter for more information on the Grand Tableau, which can be used in both systems, though the Lenormand houses must be replaced with those of the Kipper.) If the questioner is asking about their career, for example, they can seek out the Work card and look at the story that fits around it, noticing where it sits in relation to the Significator. If it is in front, then they are on top of relevant jobs, but if it is behind, work might have become overwhelming or certain aspects are proving difficult.

Tip

- The farther away a card is placed from the Significator in a large reading, the less impact it will have. Those cards closer to the Significator will have greater significance.
- Cards that appear in the rows above the Significator are still under consideration and are part of the thought process, whereas cards beneath are things that the questioner has control over.
- Cards ahead of the Significator are more manageable than those that have been placed behind it.

Magic of Kipper Cards

The Kipper cards have been
growing in popularity, and
more readers are discovering
how its situational cards reflect
the modern world. There is
a selection of packs available,
though not all will contain the
directional clues spoken about
here or display the groupings. The
Rainbow Kipper was designed
with the new Kipper reader in
mind. Unlike the tarot, where our
intuition plays an important part
in deciphering the message, the
Kipper is heavily dependent on the

system itself for accuracy. A new reader can certainly begin to read the cards
with the information provided in this book, but if you wish to deepen your
understanding and practice, you may want to look for a more in-depth guide
devoted just to this system.

Start small. Place a few cards into different scenarios and consider how the
stories change when the cards are placed in different sequences and orders.
The more you practice, the greater your awareness will become and the more
accurate your readings will become.

3

PLAYING CARDS

Even today, the magic of playing cards as a tool for divination continues to inspire the cartomancer. This could be due to the familiar nature of playing-card symbols, and the fact that such a common household object might hold secrets the layperson is unaware of. This is certainly why some people who live in conservative parts of the world might choose playing cards over other forms of divination; they draw less attention to the reader. A table of playing cards in a café is unlikely to draw attention, whereas a tarot deck might arouse concern or fear in those who are not accustomed to seeing them.

As with the tarot, the history of playing cards is shrouded in mystery, as nobody knows exactly where they originated or when. There are mentions of playing cards being used in gaming starting in about 1377 in Europe. Card games were popular in China, Persia (the ancient Iranian empire that was based in western Asia), and India before this, but aside from the Mamluk cards that date from the same period and were discovered in the Turkish city of Istanbul in 1939, most cannot be easily compared to the European decks that we use today. By the late fifteenth century, gaming with cards had become so popular that the Church was unable to stop everyday people from finding some and using them.

By the sixteenth century, cards were being used for divination and prediction, though it is impossible to know how and when this started. Though other tools, such as tarot and Lenormand cards, have become popular in recent years, playing cards have never fallen out of favor. Elaborate designs are now available, some with fortune-telling in mind, but the accessibility of a regular playing card deck never ceases to fascinate. It could be because there is far more to it than meets the eye, or perhaps the surprising fact that such simple designs can transmit such accurate and precise messages. While there has never been any evidence found to suggest that the cards were invented for any reason other than to play games, a deck of playing cards holds a surprising amount of information within its simple design.

Structure and a Surprising Discovery

A deck of playing cards comprises fifty-two cards, plus two joker cards, which are rarely if ever used. The deck is split into four suits, which are hearts, spades, clubs, and diamonds. Within each suit are ten numbered cards (or pips) and three court cards, which are jack, queen, and king. Aside from the courts and aces, the traditional deck is pretty unspectacular, though still attractive. The emblems for each suit are colored in either red (hearts and diamonds) or black (spades and clubs).

What is not immediately noticeable is that the deck appears to have a calendar encoded within it. You may have already noted that the card deck has fifty-two cards, which is the same number of weeks in a year, and that the four suits could correspond to the four seasons. The thirteen cards in each suit highlight the thirteen weeks in each season, and the thirteen lunar cycles in a year. If this is not enough to convince you, should you count all of the numbers up in the deck, counting the aces as one, then the twos, threes and so on, including the jacks as eleven, the queens as twelve, and the kings as thirteen. These add up to 364 days, and there are 364 days in a fixed lunar year (a year based on the monthly cycles of the moon's phases).

Traditional Meanings

One of the differences between this divination tool and those already mentioned is that there is no definitive guide to how the cards should be interpreted. In fact, you can read manuals by five different playing-card diviners, and each will likely offer a unique directory of meanings. While there may be a slight difference in cultural responses to the symbols within the Lenormand cards, most people accept that the Dog symbolizes loyalty and the Ring is a token of love, but the interpretations of a deck of playing cards are hugely diverse. Over the past 700 years, a huge variety of personal reading styles have been handed down through families and from teachers, which means no one method or list of definitions has greater authority over the next.

It can take some time to find a method of reading playing cards that will suit you, and it is important to remember that not all systems will. Most styles of reading adopt a method similar to that popularized by the Lenormand, where cards are read in groups. The first card in the line will hold the greatest strength and each card that follows will add shape and texture to the interpretation. Let's take a look at one of the most widely used meanings for the cards and some examples of how you might read them, but again, this information is not more accurate or authoritative than any other.

Numerological and Elemental System

One way of reading playing cards is to look at the number on the card in conjunction with the element associated with each suit. What follows is an accepted overview of the meanings for numbers in relation to cartomancy, but once again, there are many views on what numbers mean. I advise you to keep exploring until you find a technique that resonates for you or invent your own.

One

The one (or ace) is often reserved for new beginnings and fresh starts in cartomancy. Being the first real number, the potential of the suit is held within it like a seed. Therefore, it could concern an opportunity or fresh spark of inspiration.

Two

Twos concern duality. They often depict a relationship between two things, and cards with this number can be seen to describe relationships and interactions between people. Choice is also part of the two, as it presents two options.

Three

The number three is associated with growth and expansion, making it a fertile number that is related to births of all kinds. This could concern the birth of a child but may also talk of something that has been created, nurtured, or grown.

Four

The four is a stable number, representing foundation. It is not fluid like the numbers already mentioned because it speaks of order and control. It is a token of security. In some cases, it can inhibit growth and represent immobility.

Five

Difficulties arise with this number because it breaks up the stability of the four. Therefore, cards with the number five can predict problems or a wrench in the works. Disorganization, chaos, and insecurity are characteristics of the number five, but we must also remember that it releases us from the stodgy nature of the number four.

Six

The sixes are balanced cards that can represent harmony, peace, and the assistance of others. For this reason, the number can sometimes speak of community issues.

Seven

Challenges are presented by the number seven. These are slightly different to those represented by the number five, since experience is part of this number's makeup. Cards with this number depict strength that has been gained and tests of our ability to handle problems.

Eight

The number eight is associated with maturity and mastery. This is a confident number that can suggest accomplishment. The challenges of the number seven have been overcome, and the person receiving these cards is heading toward the finish line.

Nine

Because the nine is the last real number, it is often considered the completion of a situation. These cards highlight the culmination or finalization of something.

Ten

The ten is a transitional number, suggesting the beginning of a new cycle. Something has ended but the person receiving these cards will have been transformed by the experience.

Court Cards

The court cards are not associated with particular numbers, though they do grow in maturity through ranking.

JACK

A jack is generally perceived as an inexperienced person or youth. As the youngest court, he (or she, since it describes young people of both genders) is energetic and passionate.

QUEEN

A queen is a mature female-identifying person. She is nurturing and wise, encompassing feminine traits and wisdom.

KING

A king is a mature male-identifying person. He is practical and authoritative, displaying masculine traits, leadership, and mastery.

Elements

Which elements should be associated with which suits is much contested, but readers are advised to work with associations that make personal sense when creating their own system. Here is what I find to be a logical way of looking at the suits.

Suit	Correspondences	Element
Hearts	Emotions, feelings, romance, love	Water
Spades	Thoughts, communication, ideas	Air
Clubs	Energy, enthusiasm, passion, sex	Fire
Diamonds	Money, work, material concerns	Earth

Bringing Everything Together

Combining number and element is one way of constructing your own keywords. For example, when mixing the number one and the element of water in the ace of hearts, we could be looking at a new love. The combination of the number nine and the element of earth in the nine of diamonds suggests a job well done. In a reading, this could mean retirement or a financial reward.

When learning, it is advisable to buy a couple of decks since they are so inexpensive. One deck can be used as your learning deck, and you can write the keywords and a few of the meanings on the faces of the cards.

Combination with Court Cards

The court cards are combined in the same way as the rest of the numbers. A jack, as an example, would represent a younger person of either gender, who is enthusiastic or, in some cases, inexperienced. The queen and king represent mature adults who are masters within their suits. Their traits are a combination of their femininity or masculinity with their element. The hearts and diamonds would be considered feminine and receptive suits, and the spades and clubs are masculine and active, so a card such as the queen of hearts would be softer in nature than the queen of spades.

The following list is not exhaustive, but it will stimulate the intuition of the reader:

JACK OF HEARTS

A young or inexperienced lover, a kind-hearted child, a sensitive soul, a dreamer

JACK OF SPADES

Curious youth, witty, a spy, someone whom you may need to be cautious around

JACK OF CLUBS

A thrill seeker, a fun friend, impulsive, a sexual liaison, active, adventurer

JACK OF DIAMONDS

Athletic, strong minded, committed, a saver of money, an entrepreneur, sensible

QUEEN OF HEARTS

Romantic, an affectionate friend, flirtatious, giddy, a trustworthy friend, empathic

QUEEN OF SPADES

An intelligent woman, intellectual, honest, educated, straight-talking

QUEEN OF CLUBS

A socialite, enjoys luxury, sensual, a passionate lover, creative, flirty

QUEEN OF DIAMONDS

Practical, organized, a loyal spouse, career minded, good with money

KING OF HEARTS

Compassionate, level-headed, emotional advisor, romantic lover, a father figure, approachable, wise

KING OF SPADES

Ambitious, public speaker, controlled, arrogant, can be harsh in his views, fair, intelligent, knowledgeable

KING OF CLUBS

A leader, an influencer, enjoys luxury and praise, sexually driven

KING OF DIAMONDS

Secure, a financial investor, financially stable, businessperson, successful, enjoys the good life

Reading the Cards

There are many ways in which playing cards can be read, and there are lots of elaborate spreads. However, with all forms of cartomancy, keeping things small and simple to begin with is often the best option. Finding a method or spread that suits you is vital while practicing and becoming familiar with the cards. A three-card spread can reveal a lot of information without overwhelming the new reader, so I've provided a selection of possible three-card layouts for you to explore. Before beginning your reading, it is advisable to find a space and time when you are unlikely to be disturbed. Shuffling the cards is personal to each reader. Some will perform a simple hand-over-hand shuffle, but if you prefer to swirl them around on the table, that is just as good. Whatever method feels

comfortable for you is advisable. Tweaks to these reading options can be made if you are reading for a specific question:

- Past / Present / Future
- Situation / Obstacle / Advice
- Option 1 / Option 2 / Guidance
- Situation / Action / Outcome
- Strengths / Weaknesses / Solution
- What to do / What not to do / Outcome

The more proficient you become, the more cards you can add to each position. For example, you can draw two cards for one position and fuse their meanings, with the second card enhancing the first. So for example, if the jack of hearts was drawn first, followed by the two of spades, the reader might   intuit that this *young lover* wishes to *speak* from his heart since this jack is romantic and the two of spades concerns communication.

Developing Your Own Meanings

If you don't find a system that meets your needs, you can always develop your own, which is something readers have been doing for hundreds of years. One way of doing this is to think of fifty-two different words and assign them to each of the playing cards. When these keywords arise in a reading, they can be combined to provide a message. Should you decide that the ace of spades represents endings (a popular definition with many readers) and that the six of hearts is a journey, then when you read the two together, you may foresee a trip that will be canceled.

Take time to really look at the faces of the cards and the arrangement of the pips (the symbols of the suits on a card). You might notice how the six symbols on the six of hearts are grouped into two sets of three and this might reinforce the meaning of emotional balance and harmony.

How to Bring the Magic of the Playing Cards into Your Life

Because playing cards are inexpensive and easy to come by, you could draw on the cards themselves, creating symbols or simple pictures to remind you of the card meanings and to help you tap straight into your intuition. Lay the cards out and play with them often, because the more you do this, the stronger your link with this divination tool will become.

4

ELDER FUTHARK RUNES

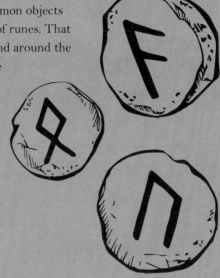

Micromancy is the name given to divination with small objects, and the most common objects diviners use are the different varieties of runes. That said, most small objects that you can find around the home can be gathered together to make a divinatory tool, as you will see in various chapters of this book.

In this chapter, we will start by taking look at a handful of different rune systems, examining their history and popular meanings. After that, methods for reading and spreads will be discussed in a little more detail.

Rune History

The runes are an ancient alphabet system that was used by the Germanic and Nordic people of northern Europe, and it is said that they are two thousand years old. The word *rune* derives from the Old High German *runa*, meaning "a secret" or "mystery." The letters of the runic alphabet, which could be used to spell out words of power, were carved onto weapons and amulets as well as used for divination.

Centuries after the runes were said to have originated, they were claimed by the Vikings and dispersed around the world. As with many tools of divination, the runes were shunned by the Church, which linked them to witchcraft. They went out of favor as a result, but interest in them resurfaced in the nineteenth century, and their magic continues to enchant today.

The oldest complete runic alphabet in existence is called the Elder Futhark, which is so named for the first six runes (Fehu to Kaunaz). Over time, the people and the runes evolved, meaning that newer alphabets came into existence. The Younger Futhark has only sixteen letters within it, and Northumbrian Futhark, which includes elements of Celtic culture, grew in size to thirty-three. The Elder Futhark is the most common, however, probably due to the relevance of its symbols and how they correspond to the seasons, the days of the week, and the directions of a compass.

While not as well-known for divination as cards, runes are a popular choice for many diviners. They can be made from a variety of materials—most commonly wood or stone—and these objects are cast by lightly throwing a random handful onto a clean, flat surface. There are various casting boards and cloths that you can buy or make. These are typically divided into different sections that give runes a specific context, depending on where they should fall on the board or cloth during a reading. How a rune falls is also important, because if the rune symbol appears upside down, there may be a reverse meaning for it. Most runes are one-sided, so it is likely that one or more will fall face down and the rune will not be visible. Many diviners choose to disregard these runes in a reading, either considering their messages as not yet relevant or better ignored.

You can also read runes by drawing them one by one and laying them out in predetermined spreads for static readings, much like in cartomancy. Reversals are interpreted the same way for set layouts as they are in castings.

Structure

We will be going over the Elder Futhark since it is both the oldest and most popular runic alphabet. It is divided into three distinct groups, each named after a Norse god: Freya's aett, Hagal's aett, and Tyr's aett. There are eight runes in each aett. Each rune has its own meaning, and each of the twenty-four runes is equal in value. It is important to note that some practitioners include what is called the "blank rune," but this is a modern addition and not part of the ancient sequence.

> ### Tip
>
> Many but not all the runes have a reversed meaning, due to the fact that some of them look the same either way up.

Freya's Aett

This group deals with creation and the beginning of time, therefore it addresses growth, fertility, and new beginnings.

FEHU (CATTLE)

Fehu is the rune of luxury and abundance, due to the association between cattle and wealth in the ancient world. It can signify prosperity within business, but because it is the first in the set, it is also a rune of new beginnings. When it arrives in a reading, it suggests that better times are ahead.

Reversed: financial difficulties, loss of fortune

URUZ (AUROCHS)

Uruz is connected to the now-extinct aurochs, which was a species of wild cattle, and indicates great strength. The power and courage of this rune suggest that you are able to overcome obstacles. However, responsibility comes with power, and you may be asked to choose your battles wisely.

Reversed: fatigue, weakness, domination

THURISAZ (THORN)

Thurisaz is associated with sharp objects and the bite of a serpent, therefore it can be viewed as a warning regarding those who might be out to deceive you. It also suggests that a move you intend to make could be risky. With this in mind, planning a defense is advised so that you are prepared for any surprise attacks or threats.

Reversed: stubbornness, caution needed

ANSUZ (GOD, DIVINE)

Ansuz is concerned with communication that may be from divine sources, so the messages you pick up from the world around you every day may seem random or coincidental, but they can also have an important personal meaning. This rune is also associated with sage advice, suggesting that you may be getting wise counsel from an experienced person.

Reversed: communication problems, disconnection

RAIDO (TRAVEL)

Raido is a rune of movement, and it predicts a journey, but while the trip could be physical, it is more likely a metaphorical one or the start of a new interest. Developments of all kinds are hinted at, and when this rune is drawn, it reminds you of the discipline and determination that you need to reach a goal. Now is not the time to stay still, so making a move is vital.

Reversed: delays, disruptions to travel or plans

KAUNAZ (TORCH, FLAME)

While the primary meaning of this rune is knowledge, the image of a flame is also linked to passion. This might be the passion or physical attraction shared by two people, but it could also represent a passionate interest in a subject or situation. When this rune is drawn, the warmth of enthusiasm and new understanding are represented.

Reversed: loss of love, ignorance

GEBO (GENEROSITY, GIFTS)

Gebo is connected to sharing, so it can represent a time when we give and receive generous gifts, and the rune can also describe charity. You may be on the receiving end of generosity when this rune appears, but it might also be asking what you have that you can share, donate, or surprise someone else with. Not all gift-giving includes physical things—a phone call or compliment could lift someone else's day.

Reversed: no reversed meaning

WUNJO (JOY, HAPPINESS)

Wunjo is associated with happiness and contentment. If read as a rune for the future, it could be the "happily ever after" rune, but it usually suggests a feeling of gratitude for where you are in life or for being in a specific situation. A fulfilling relationship, good friendships, and an overall feeling of satisfaction are described when this rune is pulled.

Reversed: emotional worries, distrust, dissatisfaction

Hagal's Aett

This group deals with darker and more disruptive topics. The situations described here are often external rather than internal, suggesting that something we can't control is going to bring difficulty and challenges.

HAGALAZ (HAIL)

Hagalaz is a rune of disruptive energy. It is associated with bad weather, so it foretells stormy events and disorder of all kinds. It is likely that little can be done when Hagalaz blows its way into a reading other than repair the damage after it has blown itself out and rebuild. It is often advisable to sit tight and make sure you are as secure as you can be for a while.

Reversed: no reversed meaning

NAUTHIZ (NEED)

Nauthiz is the rune of necessity and suggests hardship or a time of need. This can lead to frustration and feeling restricted, since your needs are not always met. Eventual luck is hinted at, so if you wait patiently, a silver lining will appear and you may end up stronger as a result.

Reversed: no reversed meaning

ISA (ICE)

Isa freezes a situation, suggesting that something will be blocked or delayed. For relationships, it could predict a period of cooling off or temporary separation (isolation), potentially resulting from conflict. Isa is a slow-moving rune, and it can suggest it will take time before things are resolved.

Reversed: no reversed meaning

JERA (HARVEST, YEAR)

Jera is the rune of harvest, suggesting the result of hard work. Concerning cycles and a twelve-month period (Jera is the twelfth rune), it denotes successful completion and endings. While the rewards of a good harvest can be enjoyed, new beginnings are also connected to the meaning, so it is important to remember that a new cycle will soon begin.

Reversed: no reversed meaning

EIHWAZ (YEW TREE)

When Eihwaz falls into a reading, the rune suggests progress. This does not mean quick turnarounds but rather that persistence and endurance are necessary. Since yew trees are often found around graveyards, there is also a connection to death and endings, suggesting that it could be important for you to clear out people, situations, and things that are no longer needed as you work toward your desired goal.

Reversed: no reversed meaning

PERTHO (CUP)

Pertho is connected to mysteries and the unknown. It is said that if the rune is drawn alone or at the beginning of a reading, the oracle is showing that the answer is not meant to be known just yet and that the reading must stop. If pulled later in a sequence, however, it could suggest secrets to be revealed. Accessing the unknown is part of divination, so this rune also asks that you heed your intuition and trust your gut.

Reversed: loss of control, being out of touch with your intuition

ALGIZ (ELK, SEDGE)

You might see the connection between this rune and the antlers of the elk or the prickly edges of a leaf—the features that keep them safe. As a rune of protection, it can safeguard family and loved ones, but it might also concern the protective eye of a deity, since it is often associated with the higher realms.

Reversed: a need for protection, vulnerability

SOWELO (SUN, EAGLE)

Sowelo is the rune of the sun, suggesting warmth, fertility, and fortune. Its brightness can influence runes around it, and it means that a dark period will be coming to an end. In a reading, it is a predictor of success and achievement and can, in some cases, highlight the truth like a lightning flash. Places where the sun shines are also noted for the traveler.

Reversed: no reversed meaning

Tyr's Aett

The final group concerns earthly and material matters. It corresponds to our society and our integration with the world and people around us.

TIWAZ (STAR, SPEAR)

Tiwaz is the rune of the warrior, so it is naturally connected to those times when you must stand your ground or fight. Courage and victory are important aspects of this rune's meaning, but so is justice. If you are intending to stand up for yourself in conflict, then this rune reminds you that fairness will prevail. Make sure that your conscience is clear, because this rune will reveal anything that is less than honorable.

Reversed: dishonorable actions, unfairness

BERKANO (BIRCH TREE, SWAN)

Berkano is the rune of birth and is therefore often linked to pregnancy and growth. This is not only about the birth of children, though, because new projects, relationships, or finances are all shown by this rune. This is the rune of the caregiver, but it can also signify self-care. If you have not been looking after your own health and you need to kickstart a better diet or exercise regime, then this rune may well turn up in your reading.

Reversed: health issues, infertility, growth problems

EHWAZ (HORSE)

Ehwaz is the rune of travel, and it can describe all kinds of journeys, business trips, and future vacations, in addition to relocation. Whereas Raido (the other rune associated with travel) describes the inner or spiritual path, Ehwaz concerns physical movement, so it can speed up a situation or suggest a trip of some kind. In some cases, it will remind the questioner that help from others will aid progress. Vehicles of all types are noted.

Reversed: car trouble, travel delays

MANNAZ (HUMANKIND, SELF)

As a rune of humanity, Mannaz is of the collective but also of the self. It reminds us of our fellow humans and those things that we all share. Therefore, this rune can be associated with compassion and understanding, encouraging us to think about the things we can share with others. When the rune is drawn, it might suggest a little self-evaluation and ask that you consider your own purpose and how you relate to the world around you. New decisions are part of this process.

Reversed: inability to self-analyze, selfishness

LAGUZ (WATER)

Laguz is associated with water and, therefore, to emotions. While it can suggest moving with the flow of life, it relates to a range of different feelings you might have. Tears are naturally connected to this as a method of cleansing and moving forward, but the rune is also a strong omen for love. In a relationship reading, it can suggest that even the stormiest of unions can find resolution and that new love could be around the corner.

Reversed: unemotive, difficult emotions

INGUZ (EARTH, BOAR)

Inguz is connected to sexuality and male sexuality in particular. However, it will turn up in a reading to signify all kinds of sexuality and the passion involved in relationships, regardless of gender identification. Berkano is associated with feminine sexuality and reproduction, but this card speaks of the seed, thus it is also a symbol of new beginnings and of getting things started.

Reversed: no reversed meaning

OTHILA (NOBILITY, LAND)

There is a homey feel to this rune, since it is linked to the family, our ancestors, and those things we have inherited. This does not necessarily mean possessions but rather family traits or childhood nurturing. Whereas this rune is associated with tradition and the way things have always been done, in some circumstances it will question whether striking out from family expectations and tradition might be more beneficial.

Reversed: disloyalty, cutting ties with tradition

DAGAZ (DAWN, SAGE)

Dagaz is the rune for day and light, and it can be a welcome omen for those currently going through a "dark night of the soul" or a difficult period. As with the rising of the sun each day, this rune symbolizes hope, alerting the questioner to a brighter future. With this in mind, it can provide clarity, hinting that a solution to a problem will soon be found. A breakthrough could be imminent, as this rune hints at the improvement of a situation.

Reversed: no reversed meaning

Reading the Runes

The runes can be read in a variety of ways, but drawing them and placing them in a set layout or casting (throwing) a handful are the most popular. In the layout method, the runes can be pulled randomly, one by one, from a bag and placed into the chosen layout. You need to be observant of whether a rune is pulled upright or reversed (upside down) before it is added to the reading.

To cast runes, a white cloth (white symbolizing a pure intention) is laid down, and a small handful of runes is lightly thrown onto the surface. The diviner uses intuition to determine the importance of where the runes fall. Runes that are closer together may have special significance, whereas those at a distance could have a weaker meaning or could foretell situations occurring further into the future. Runes that land facedown, so you can't see the rune symbol, should be disregarded as they are either not yet relevant or better off ignored.

Some readers will use a specially designed sheets for reading. These sheets are divided into different areas. You will find more about spreads and casting sheets on page 66–69.

Creating Your Own Runes

There are many ornate and beautifully designed runes that you can buy, including plastic sets that are mass-produced as well as sets that are handcrafted using different crystals, metals, or wood. It is easy to find runes online, but it's worth visiting New Age shops to find a set that feels right for you. The feel of the runes is of great importance. A diviner might not want a set that is too small or may prefer the weight of stones over wood.

Most experienced rune casters advise that a diviner creates their own set. This can be as easy or as involved as you wish. Some people take some sea pebbles and draw on them with a marker, where others will find a discarded branch and cut it into disks before burning or carving the runic symbols into them. Neither way is better, but taking something natural and creating your own runes is an accepted and preferred option for many, as it charges the objects with your own energy and intention. Small wooden discs can be bought in craft shops for next to nothing, and these are a great option too.

Rune cards are also an option, and there are many that don't cost much to buy. Rather than a stone or wooden disc, packs of cards have been designed with a runic symbol on each. The benefit is that these can have complex

Tip

You will need something to hold your runes inside to keep them safe. Most opt for a drawstring bag or some kind of pouch. These are both easy to find or make. Most containers will work but bear in mind that the runes will need to be concealed when mixed and that the box or bag should be big enough to fit a hand comfortably.

illustrations on them that provide cues to help you remember the meaning of the runes. With the rune Wunjo, as an example, the designer can add images of joy and fulfillment to the card, as well as helpful keywords. This is something that can be easily replicated at home by cutting twenty-four cards out of cardstock or heavy paper.

Whatever form of runes you choose, there are a few things worth considering. Each object must be of similar size and shape so that differences among them are not easily detected when drawing from your rune bag or deck of cards. They must also be large enough to contain each symbol easily. If you are painting onto a stone or surface, will it require some kind of protection to keep the image intact? If you are using a wood-burning device, care is needed to prevent hurting yourself or risking a fire or damaging property. Make sure that you seek advice and read the instructions for any tools before use.

5

WITCHES' RUNES

In comparison to the more popular runic alphabets, such as the Elder Futhark, the alphabet of the Witches' Runes is significantly smaller, comprising just thirteen runes. Thirteen is the number of witches traditionally in a coven, but it also corresponds to the twelve astrological signs plus the final Eye rune, which encompasses the energy of the previous twelve. Like traditional runes, they are simple in design, and the symbols are typically painted onto identical, small tokens. The runic symbols themselves, however, are not the same as those we find in the Germanic alphabet, and have their own unique meanings.

As with many methods of divination, the history of the Witches' Runes is not complete. It is likely that they evolved from sacred writings in the Middle East and were at some point carved onto amulets and stones by European Romani. They believed this gave them power, in much the same way people believed the Germanic runes did. The Witches' Runes are also said to have a long association with divination.

One of the benefits of working with Witches' Runes is that their symbols are easier to identify and remember than those in the Germanic alphabet. For example, the Sun, Moon, and Star are simple renderings of each of those astronomical bodies, and the Crossroads shows two double-ended arrows, one intersecting the other so they point in the four cardinal directions.

The Thirteen Runes of Power

The Sun

The Sun is a positive rune, bringing new beginnings and bold, positive change. It represents achievement and recognition, so progress is certain for the receiver of this rune. Warmth and success are characteristics of its energy.

The Moon

The Moon conceals more than it reveals, meaning that this rune suggests things operating behind the scenes are not yet acknowledged or understood by the questioner. The rune indicates emotional issues, along with imagination and intuitive gifts. The feminine connotation of this symbol is also important, possibly suggesting a wise elder female.

Flight

The birdlike shapes represent Flight, so the rune is associated with movement and, therefore, travel of all kinds. The rune could describe a journey, but the idea of the bird as a carrier of information is also part of this stone's meaning, making it a token of communication. News could arrive when this rune falls into a reading.

Rings

This rune shows three joined rings and is a symbol of connection. This could concern the coming together of people or the combining of more than one thing to make something different. In our modern day, social media might be an example of a tool that allows people to interact and share.

Romance

The Romance rune speaks of love and relationships, suggesting deep commitment and desire. It will turn up to illustrate significant bonds, but when the questioner is not asking about their love life, it can signify important business unions or mergers. Soul mates and harmonious relationships of all kinds are connected to this rune.

Woman

The Woman rune might depict an important woman in the life of the questioner, but it also speaks about characteristics that are traditionally feminine in nature, such as nurturing, compassion, homemaking, and the maternal role. Pregnancy can sometimes be predicted.

Man

The Man rune can refer to relevant men in the life of the questioner, but it also highlights personalities that are particularly masculine in nature. Whereas the Woman rune is passive, the Man rune suggests action. This stone is associated with a provider, protection, and authority. It sometimes shows up as the father figure in the questioner's life.

Harvest

Harvest suggests the fruits of one's labor, and it depicts the results of hard work and effort. While it will undoubtedly deliver the profit of an investment, it also reminds us that we will get out what we put in to something. This is an extremely fortuitous rune, offering positive benefits for the questioner.

Crossroads

The Crossroads rune provides options. An important decision may need to be made, and this rune reminds the questioner that now is the time to make it, however difficult. While life might not be easy, the upside of making such a choice is the experience that is gained from taking a conscious step forward and of new understanding and strength.

The Star

The Star is often considered a symbol of guidance and hope within divination and fortune-telling. This rune reminds questioners of their dreams and goals, and the runes closest to it in a reading will help to identify which of the questioner's dreams could hold promise. This is an inspiring rune, which could help those in a rut or feeling lost to find renewed purpose.

Waves

The Waves are connected to movement, and those things that cannot always be controlled. Sometimes we must simply go with the flow and accept that not everything can be influenced or controlled. Sometimes we must fix what we can but realize that there might be bigger events in motion that we are unaware of right now. With this in mind, the Waves rune can reflect the questioner's insecurity and doubts with regard to specific situations.

The Scythe

The Scythe is a popular divinatory symbol that represents endings and death. When this rune enters a reading, it is likely that something is over. The questioner may know what this is about, and the ending might have already happened, or it may be in progress at the time of the reading. In some readings, however, the rune suggests that the questioner should put an end to something that is no longer serving them. Some diviners will also see the Scythe as a warning of imminent danger, though this needn't be as severe as it sounds.

The Eye

The final rune is the Eye, and it is a symbol of the truth, representing clarity and removing doubt. The questioner will soon be able to see things for what they are, and the unknown will soon become known. In some cases, it will be linked to intuition, but the rune usually suggests a new awareness regarding something or someone.

Tip

The instructions for creating your own runes (pages 54–55) and casting them (pages 53–54) work just as well for the Witches' Runes as they do for the Elder Futhark.

Working with Witches' Runes

While it might seem as though the small size of the Witches' Runes set means they are not as substantial as other systems, this is not necessarily so. How you use them is very much up to you, but they do work well in pairs. Should two (or even three) fall together when casting, they will naturally unite. The following examples suggest ways in which some pairs could be read, but interpretations are not limited to these ideas. Note that the change in order can affect the interpretation.

Examples of Witches' Rune Pairings

Runes	Possible Interpretation
Woman + Romance	A loving female partner, a committed woman
Man + Moon	A secretive male
Moon + Man	A secret about a man
Waves + Scythe	A quick ending, a last-minute cancellation
Flight + Sun	Good news, successful trip, a warm destination for a vacation
Moon + Eye	Deception is revealed, a solution, end of confusion or doubt
Crossroads + Rings	Seeking advice from others, teamwork during a time of trials
Rings + Crossroads	Difficulties in partnerships, issues about marriage or commitment
Woman + Harvest	A successful female, a businesswoman, an educated lady
Flight + Romance	A romantic weekend away, a fast-moving relationship
Star + Romance	A dream lover, unrealistic expectations of love

❋ ❋ ❋

6

CASTING
CHARMS

You may think that the charms that you see on bracelets or pendants are a recent invention, but this is far from the truth. Charms, in one way or another, have been used since the Neolithic era (which started in 10,000 BCE), when they were often fashioned from shells, pieces of bone, or clay. Intricate charm bracelets have been found at archaeological sites and are believed to have been used to protect against negative energy or to encourage health and prosperity.

Not unlike the runes, early charms were made of wood or stone with symbols engraved on them, but there is evidence from the Bronze Age of these materials being carved into specific shapes. These protective and powerful amulets would eventually become popular in the Middle Ages, and kings and queens would wear them when going into battle, while knights would wear them on their belts to secure success in a fight. Later on, Queen Victoria was known to wear gold charms, often connected to her family and her husband, Prince Albert. After his death, these charms would contain pieces of his hair and portraits of him.

In the 1950s and 1960s, charm bracelets became popular gifts to give to teenage girls. A bracelet with a few charms would act as a starter, and the person receiving the gift would either buy charms to represent their own likes or to commemorate events, such as a milestone birthday. Lately, there has been a resurgence in charm bracelets, and some of these charms have found their way onto the fortune-teller's table in addition to the wrists of style-conscious young ladies.

Shapes and Meanings

Most charms you see today have a well-known shape—teddy bear, heart, scales, anchor, key, etc.—which gives them easily recognized symbolic importance. Pulling a mermaid might foretell temptation and destruction, whereas a butterfly could indicate transformation. Charms are quite easy to come by, and you can buy inexpensive packs of fifty or a hundred charms online, giving you a large variety of symbols.

A charm set can include as many charms as you like, and there are no rules as to what you can and cannot include. However, it does make sense to put together a balanced set, offering warnings as well as positive omens. Storing them in a drawstring bag is a good way to keep them safe, and it makes drawing them for readings easy. The following list is a guide to such a collection.

Charm	Symbolism
Airplane	Air travel, quick movement
Anchor	Dependability, restriction, lack of movement, burden
Apple	Temptation, seduction
Book	Education, information, instruction, secrets
Boot	Grounding, practicality, standing up for oneself
Butterfly	Change, transformation, metamorphosis
Camera	Memories, the past
Cane	Support, assistance
Clover	Luck, fortune, favor
Crown	Power, honor, ego
Dog	Loyalty, faithfulness, friendship
Envelope	Messages, mail, information
Feather	A sign from a loved one in spirit
Heart	Love, warmth, romance
Hot-Air Balloon	Perspective, rising above something
Jigsaw Piece	Something is missing, a problem, not fitting in
Key	Solutions, an answer will soon come, initiation, acceptance

Charm	Symbolism
Lock	Security, stability, safety, feeling imprisoned
Mask	Dishonesty, shady person, distrust, trickster
Moon	Mystery, the unknown, the subconscious
Owl	Wisdom, knowledge, good advice
Purse	Money, finances, spending, accounts
Rabbit	Birth, fertility
Scales	Justice, fairness, unbiased advice, balance
Scissors	To cut something away, sever ties
Ship	Sea travel, cruise, long trip, vacation
Skull	Endings, death, completion, finality
Snake	A warning, an opponent, gossip
Spider	Hard work, effort, endurance, persistence
Star	Hope, inspiration, belief, guidance
Stroller	Children, pregnancy, starting a family
Sun	Prosperity, good health and well-being, vitality
Teapot	Get-togethers with friends, social gatherings, taking a break
Tree	Growth, family connections, ancestors

Casting Small Objects

The One-Object Draw

The easiest and simplest way of obtaining an answer
from your charms is to pull one from your bag. Focus
on your question then shake the bag a little, put your
hand inside, and take one charm at random. If you wish
to know about the potential for a forthcoming romantic
relationship, rather than asking, "When will I next have
a relationship?" you would do better to ask, "What do
I need to do if I want a new relationship?" The Skull charm might suggest that
you need to recover from a previous relationship before starting a new one.

Spreads

Runes, crystals, and charms can be read in spreads. A spread is simply a layout with
predetermined meanings for its positions, and each item is drawn one by one and
placed into position. This is a simple and effective way of reading objects, because
both the object you draw and the position it goes in will spark your intuition.

Spreads can be created to involve any subject, but it is often a good idea to
have a few basic ones up your sleeve. For instance, the snapshot spread shown
here looks at the different areas of a person's life through the lens of the present
time, which makes a good starting point for a workable life overview.

An Example of a Simple Charm Layout

In the spread example given, the Key suggests that a problem within the questioner's career will soon be solved. In their romantic life, the Rabbit indicates the growth of a relationship, but it could also represent pregnancy. This would guide the person being read for, encouraging them to consider whether or not they wish to start a family. The Tree, in the position of Money, could mean an inheritance or a significant development of finances, while the Snake warns the reader that someone in the questioner's environment might be out to cause trouble.

Casting Sheets

The casting of charms can be as simple as taking a small handful from a bag and gently tossing them onto a clean surface. You can also cast them onto

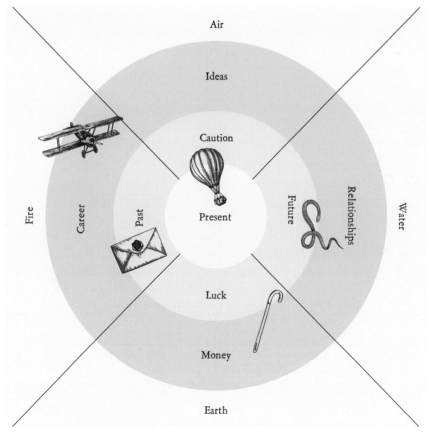

An Example of a Casting Sheet with Charms Thrown during a Reading

a sheet of paper or cloth that have areas of interest on them, such as love, career, or spirituality, as well as circles representing the past, present, and future, and spaces for the four elements. These are easy to make by simply drawing on a large sheet of paper, like the example shown here. You then just throw your charms onto the sheet. The casting sheet on the previous page shows a general layout, which is useful for someone who doesn't have a specific question.

In this example of a charm reading on a general casting sheet, you can see the following information:

Airplane in the area of Career: The person's work will take them abroad. With the airplane's tail resting on the element of fire, the work may be creative or something the questioner is passionate about. This example provides a good lesson in reading. A symbol such as this, falling into an element such as fire, could alarm a new reader or client who could be set to travel. However, it is important to not allow fear to creep into your readings. Fire can be a destructive element, but as shown here, it is also indicative of creativity and enthusiasm.

Letter in the Past section: This suggests news from someone in the questioner's past or the resolution of something that has been going on for some time.

Hot-Air Balloon in the Present: There is a need to rise above something and to gain some perspective. The charm rests on the line between Caution and Present, implying that vigilance is needed.

Cane falling on both Luck and Money: This hints at financial support that the subject should be grateful for.

Snake on both Future and Relationship: This seems to be coming toward the questioner, so having advance warning that someone coming into their life may be a gossip will be especially useful.

This next casting sheet is built around the topic of love and romance. The sections allow for the reader to look into the different areas within the questioner's love life, but it also holds a timeline (past, present, future) at its core. In this example, you can see how a romantic reading could be interpreted:

Dog in the Past suggests a reliable and faithful partner, or it could, in some circumstances, describe a loyal friend whom you could become involved with romantically.

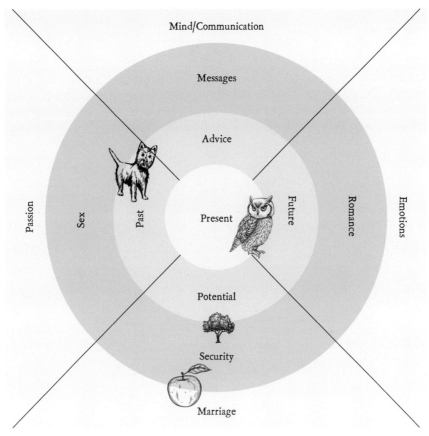

An Example of a Love Casting Sheet with Charms Thrown during a Reading

Owl in the Present (and slightly crossing into the Future position) concerns wisdom gained from previous experiences that will be carried into future relationships.

Apple in Marriage would indicate a flirtation with the idea of a more committed partnership but could also indicate that you may not be ready to settle down just yet. In the romantic reading of a married person, this symbol could suggest the temptation to be unfaithful.

Tree in Security asks the seeker to consider getting to know a potential partner before making any significant commitment or becoming carried away by their emotions.

❋ ❋ ❋

7

DIVINING
WITH
CRYSTALS

When most people think of crystals, it's healing that immediately comes to mind. Using these natural gemstones to promote better mental, emotional, and physical health is an age-old practice that is still extremely popular today. Whether crystals are laid on different areas of the body, placed in a specific area of the home, or carried around as a powerful amulet, healing and empowerment

are probably their greatest uses. Specific crystals are advised for different issues, such as to help with anxiety or lack of confidence, for stress relief, or to help someone find love.

Using crystals for divination is less common than using them for the above reasons, though there are many practitioners who do cast crystals (sometimes called lithomancy). The diviner can make an interpretation by the way the crystals look, their color, or even how the light hits them, but it is generally accepted that a message is gained from the meanings that are associated with their healing properties. Some diviners will hold a crystal to tune into it and see how it makes them feel.

Putting together a crystal set is personal to the user, and it is dependent on their needs. In the following section, you will learn about crystals that are widely available and that you can easily incorporate into your oracle. Due to the nature of crystals, the energies of some might be harder to work with than others, and a little caution is needed. Cooler crystals might dampen your mood rather than brighten it, and there are some crystals, such as moldavite, that can affect users physically, causing headaches or nausea. While using your crystals for divination, notice how the set makes you feel. If you become uncomfortable, then maybe an adjustment needs to be made, replacing a specific stone with something different.

Amber

Colors: Yellows, golds
Association: Warmth

This sunny crystal is a token of warmth and vitality. It suggests well-being and satisfaction, so it is a welcome sign. Like a small ray of sunshine, amber predicts a good outcome and promises contentment. If you are asking about a specific person, this foretells a successful and fortunate relationship or working partnership.

Amethyst

Colors: Purple shades, lavender
Association: Intuition

When amethyst is drawn, the crystal is advising that you tune into your intuition. We all have psychic abilities, however unaware of them we might be, and you are being encouraged to tune into yours. This is a time to trust your feelings and not let yourself become swayed by doubt or the opinions of others. If you have a hunch about something, follow it.

Aventurine

Color: Green
Association: Luck

We all need a little luck, and aventurine tells you when fortune is in your favor, whether it be a well-deserved success or a coincidental sprinkle of prosperity. Aventurine suggests that the universe is on your side and is giving you a nudge. There will be times when we make our own luck, but we occasionally find ourselves in the right place at the right time. If you have drawn this stone, luck is around you, so keep your eyes and ears open for opportunity.

Bloodstone

Colors: Red and green
Association: Resilience

Strength is associated with bloodstone. When this gemstone is drawn, it can suggest that you draw on conserved energy and use it to push forward. We often have far more resilience than we believe we do, so this stone is a clarifier in a reading, reminding us that we can, and will, carry on, regardless of the opposition.

Blue Lace Agate

Color: Pale blue
Association: Peace

Blue lace agate, as depicted by its soft blue coloring, is associated with peace and the quietening of the mind. For some, it will make an appearance in a casting to suggest a quieter period on the horizon or a relaxing of challenges. It is a welcome stone for many because it can suggest a time of calm and an untroubled mind. Concerning tranquility, this crystal could be advising you to spend time in a space where you will feel safe and where you can recharge.

Tip

My friend Sasha swears by keeping a bit of blue lace agate on her computer, as it seems to calm it down and keep it working properly. She also recommends that you recharge your crystals from time to time to keep their energy working. An easy way to recharge crystals is to hold them in the smoke of an incense stick for a while and ask the universe to help them give assistance to those who need it. A quick fix for those in a hurry is to blow on the crystal while imagining the help they will be able to give to others.

Carnelian

Color: Deep orange
Association: Courage

Carnelian is the stone of inner strength. You may not feel particularly strong when you work with this crystal, but its presence in a reading is saying that you have what it takes to get through. We all have courage deep within, but we are not always sure how to summon it when needed. Carnelian suggests that your greatest treasures are set within those things that make you nervous, and that believing in yourself is essential now. This crystal is often associated with confidence and self-reliance.

Clear Quartz

Color: Transparent
Association: Focus

It might seem quite obvious that a transparent stone would concern focus, since its clear surface suggests a clear mind and clarity in general. Many people use clear quartz to unblock the mind and erase brain fog, so it makes sense that it means focus and an uncluttered mind in a reading. If you have drawn this crystal, then it is important that you set a goal or keep your mind on the job. Direction is required, and you are being asked to concentrate on those things that have the greatest priority.

Dumortierite

Colors: Navy and black
Association: Patience

Dumortierite is a crystal connected to patience and taking time. Many of us want things instantly these days, and much of the world accommodates this, but there are some things that take time. Pregnancy is one example where we can do nothing other than step back and let the process unfold naturally. You are being advised to think of the bigger picture and not to rush. If this crystal is drawn, it shows that something will take longer than you had hoped for, but that little can be done to change this.

Garnet

Colors: Red and purple
Association: Passion

This vibrant stone is often associated with red-hot passion. This is a useful stone to have in a crystal reading, since it can alert you to passionate events, possibly within your romantic life, but in readings directed toward career and pastimes, it advises you to choose to do something that drives your enthusiasm and in which you are wholeheartedly involved. This crystal will motivate exciting and new happenings.

Jade

Colors: Shades of green
Association: Abundance

Jade is an attractive, light-green stone that will relay feelings of abundance when drawn. Of course, this could relate to money and a financial boost, but depending on the question asked, it can also depict something that will arrive in large amounts. In a relationship position, it could show that a lot of love is coming your way. This stone has a neutral meaning, so it really is dependent on whether abundance is viewed favorably or not. For one person, it could mean plenty of work will be welcome (especially if it falls in an area depicting the career), but for another, too much work might be overwhelming.

Jasper

Colors: Browns, deep reds
Association: Stability

Jasper is connected with the earth and, therefore, with stability and grounding.
When the stone appears in a reading, it could highlight a grounded and secure
individual, or it might suggest that you need to find a way of connecting to
the material world more effectively. This might be useful for someone who is
overemotional or who can be easily distracted by fantasy. Jasper advises that
you get real and down to earth, but it will also arrive when physical or financial
security is of importance.

Kyanite

Colors: Shades of blue
Association: Communication

When kyanite shows up in a crystal casting, it can suggest communication.
It can foretell messages that will soon arrive, but it may also alert you to the
importance of communicating in a clear and honest manner. The coolness of
kyanite suggests clarity and expressing yourself in the best way possible. Are
you in need of opening up about something, rather than bottling it up, or could
it be time for you to stand up and speak your mind?

Lapis Lazuli

Colors: Deep blues, gold
Association: Truth

When lapis lazuli is drawn, it suggests truth. It indicates that the truth will
soon emerge in connection with a specific situation, but it could also be saying

that it is best to be honest about something. It could be important that you need to be honest with someone in your life or that you should be honest with yourself. If you have been in denial about something, it could be time to rethink and accept things for how they truly are. To surrender denial is to remove a blockage, helping you to feel better and move on.

Malachite

Color: Deep green
Association: Protection

Malachite is often used as a crystal for protection, and it can be worn in jewelry or carried when needed. As a divinatory stone, this rich green crystal encourages you to look at your boundaries. Your personal safety could be at risk, but other aspects of life could be equally as vulnerable. Safeguarding yourself against an internet attack or physical viruses is one such way that you might need to improve your defenses. When this stone arrives in a reading, you may need to check out your firewalls, finances, and property and increase any insurance that you have.

Moonstone

Color: Milky
Association: Dreams

This dreamy stone concerns your hopes and wishes, your ambitions, and those things you long for. When moonstone arrives in a casting, it reminds you of your dreams and encourages belief and action. A dream can only ever be just that unless you make plans and prepare a path toward your goals. When this crystal is drawn, you are being reminded that some dreams do come true but only when a little effort and preparation is put in.

Obsidian

Color: Black
Association: Mystery

This mysterious crystal could be likened to the shadow, as it can depict those things that are hidden. In some cases, what's hidden may be in your external world, so this stone could provide a warning. However, it also concerns those things we hide within ourselves, and which we might rather not examine. Shadowy obsidian may be asking you to confront something you would rather not acknowledge and to reap the spiritual rewards of doing so.

Rhodonite

Colors: Pink and black
Association: Anxiety

This stone is usually pink and black. On looking at it, you might consider the darker markings to represent anxiety, and the pleasant pinks to symbolize healing. When this crystal is drawn, you may be falling prey to anxiety and worry that are affecting your life, and if so, this suggests that healing or a release is needed. It is likely that you may have built something up in your mind and that you may be worrying unnecessarily. The only way to untangle yourself from its clutches is to confront it and take control. When we look fear in the face, it becomes a lot smaller.

Rose Quartz

Colors: Pale pinks
Association: Love

Rose quartz is associated with love and romance, which is hinted at by its delicate and soft color. When the stone arrives in a casting, it either alerts you to the fact that you are loved or, if appropriate, that romantic love could be forthcoming.

This will be a welcome sign for those looking for a relationship. This crystal can concern emotions, and in some readings will illustrate feelings that may or may not be reciprocated. When this crystal is drawn, know that it is a descriptor of romance and of someone who cares, so look at the other stones in your layout to determine how this is manifesting in your life.

Smoky Quartz

Color: Brown
Association: Grounding

When smoky quartz is drawn in a reading, it reminds you of your physical body. It can be easy to separate the self from the physical plane, allowing your spiritual side or even your fantasies to take over, and this stone reminds you of how important it is to keep both feet on the ground. In some situations, this will mean taking a practical approach. In others, you may be required to remain level-headed and not get carried away.

Tiger's Eye

Colors: Browns, yellows, and golds
Association: Balance

This popular stone is a harbinger of balance. It could suggest that this is exactly what you need and even that you might be feeling a little off-balance. This crystal will often arise when someone is burning the candle at both ends or someone who has neglected an important aspect of their life. If you draw tiger's eye, then take a step back and look at what might be missing. It may be time to readdress your priorities.

Turquoise

Color: Blue
Association: Wisdom

Turquoise is the crystal of wisdom. Knowledge and wisdom are quite different, because not everyone who amasses knowledge is wise. Wisdom comes from experience. In some cases, this stone will come up to alert you to the presence of a wise person in your environment. Does someone have much-needed advice to impart, or should you seek out the opinion of someone who is more experienced than you are? Generally, this crystal is a reminder that there is something to be learned from a specific situation, however difficult it might be to learn from it.

Watermelon Tourmaline

Colors: Pink and green
Association: Friendship

It is not difficult to see why such a pretty gemstone with its joyous colors is connected to friendship. Reminiscent of the watermelon it is named after, its light colors are associated with the heart. If this crystal is drawn, it alerts the reader to a friendship of relevance, suggesting that a new companion will enter your life or that an existing friend has your back. This is a positive stone, but if surrounded by challenging crystals, it might be overpowered and could suggest trouble in relationships or friends who might be less than honest.

How to Read Crystals

Reading crystals is not so different to reading other objects you cast, such as runes, but owing to the different energetic properties in each crystal, you can go a bit further. Crystals can amplify and raise your energy vibrations when you read them, meaning that intuition and even psychism can be amplified to give an extra layer of information to the reading.

Many diviners will cleanse their crystals between readings. Card readers may do the same thing by placing the cards in incense smoke to clear them, but the crystal practitioner has a few additional options at their disposal. Some will hold each crystal under running water for a minute or so, neutralizing any negative energy that may have become attached to the stone. Some diviners put their stones in saltwater, because salt is known to absorb unwanted vibrations and remove negativity. Clean seawater is a great choice, but a bowl of water with a tablespoon of your chosen salt will suffice.

> **Tip**
>
> Casting sheets can be used for divination with a variety of different objects. A charms sheet, for example, can be used for crystals or runes.

There are many ways of preparing your crystals for a reading. I recommend bathing stones in the light of the moon or using a visualization meditation. To conduct a visualization meditation, take each crystal in turn and imagine a white cleansing light surrounding and covering it. As you do this, visualize any negative energies being released. You can do this for about a minute per stone. Place your prepared crystals in a bag.

To start a reading, pull a stone randomly from the bag and look up its meaning on the previous pages. You can also go beyond the prescribed meanings to intuit for yourself what a crystal means. One of the most distinctive aspects of a crystal is its color. What does the color suggest to you? Do you feel content and positive when you look at it, or does it leave you feeling cold or detached? You may feel differently about the colors and their meanings on different days and in different readings.

Crystals are all unique. Not every piece of rose quartz will look like the next. Looking into the crystal at the natural shapes or patterns inside it is another way of deciphering information. Do you see something that triggers a thought or idea?

Finally, hold the stone in your hands and close your eyes. How do you feel? Does your own vibration change? What is the gemstone trying to tell you? Any feelings that you get during this part of the reading are important.

Once you have conducted your reading, place your crystals safely back in their bag. You can repeat the cleansing process, but this is not necessary if you are giving more than one reading. Mentally thanking the crystals for their services will be enough, giving them a gentle shake to mix them together again.

❀ ❀ ❀

8

READING COLORS

In all kinds of divinatory readings, color plays an important role since it can provoke instant feelings and arouse intuition. Color can take priority in many forms of divination. Tarot designers have worked out that the use of reds and blacks on a card such as the Devil will stimulate fear and caution, and some decks have gone as far as color-coding groups of cards to reflect the natural elements (commonly, blue for water, yellow for air, orange for fire, and green for earth). The meanings of crystals can also be determined by the shade of the stone: for instance, the pale pink of rose quartz is reflective of love and romance.

Modern Meanings Associated with Color

There are, within our modern world, colors that will provoke calm and others that provoke anxiety. For example, red is associated with danger and will, therefore, stop traffic or stop a person in their tracks. Green, on the other hand, is commonly thought of as color for movement, letting us know that it is safe to cross the road. We think of blue, in all its shades, as a color that describes

things as being cold. Depending on where you are in the world, you will have your own set of associations, but the following list is generally accepted as a way of interpreting color for divinatory purposes.

Red Warning, deterrent, anger, passion, lust, rage, danger, battle, "stop"

Green Healing, nature, growth, envy, luck, refreshing, "go"

Yellow Warmth, sunshine, well-being, intellect, thought, ideas, inspiration, clarity

Blue Cool, clean, understanding, tranquility, balance, peace

Orange Exuberance, change, warmth, health, pleasant mood

Purple Protection, royalty, mysticism, wisdom, mystery, being alone, luxury

Pink Romance, femininity, friendship, sweetness, kindness

Brown Grounding, practicality, earthiness, reliability

Black Fear, death, gloominess, negative emotions, nothingness, protection

White Innocence, purity, spirit, angels, youthfulness

Ribbon Reading

One common way of divining with color is through the art of reading ribbons. A ribbon of each color can be collected and kept in a protective bag or pouch. Some diviners will include more than one kind of ribbon for each color, as this adds a variety of lengths and textures. For a reading to work, the diviner draws a bunch of ribbons and hold them loosely in their hand. With closed eyes, the questioner picks out a few ribbons at random. If the subject sees the colors before choosing, the conscious choice will disrupt the process. The questioner can select just one ribbon, but for a more detailed reading, three or four can be

drawn. Make note of which order they are drawn, since those drawn first are likely to have greater importance. If the questioner pulls two at the same time, read them as a pair, using your intuition to interpret the significance.

On the other hand, not every diviner asks a questioner to close their eyes, because the colors that the questioner deliberately chooses shows their state of mind. Instead of disrupting the process, it's seen as part of it. The choice of ribbons can bring the subject's unconscious desires, fears, needs, and predictions of the future into focus, and this can be extremely useful to the diviner. As with so many forms of divination, there are as many ways of giving a reading as there are people giving them.

Try considering the following suggestions when reading your ribbons:

- What does the color mean to you? Pink might suggest that the questioner has love on their mind.
- Are there any ribbons that are grouped together? Purple and red could indicate that the person being read for needs to protect themselves from imminent danger.
- How does the ribbon feel? Close your eyes and feel your way around the ribbon. If it is smooth, this could denote a positive response. If all you can feel are the frays on one end, and the ribbon is pink, could it indicate that a relationship has seen better days?
- How long is the ribbon? In terms of the more negative colors, the length of the ribbon will determine how long a problem will last. This is why it can help to have different ribbons of the same color but with different lengths and textures.
- It is important that you pass any thoughts or feelings you have to the questioner. Sit with the ribbon and hold it loosely in your hand. Do any words, emotions, or pictures come into your mind? Find a way of translating these sensitively and clearly.

Spreads

When using ribbons, spreads are not read in the same way as with cards or crystals, but the result is similar. The order in which someone pulls a ribbon can equate to different points of reference. For instance, three ribbons, pulled one after another, might represent the past, present, and future.

In the following example, consider these ribbons in a mind, body, and spirit reading.

Mind ● Green — Healing is relevant as this ribbon could detect previous problems that the questioner still needs to recover from. An overactive mind or too much pressure may have resulted in this person becoming stressed and anxious. As this is the color of nature, getting out into the countryside would benefit their mental health.

Body ● Blue — Blue is the color of balance and tranquility. This might suggest that a good diet is required, and that packaged or fast food might not be good for the questioner's health. Since blue has a natural association with water, drinking water might be important, as well as swimming or maybe taking a trip to the ocean or a lake.

Spirit ● Red — Red can represent warnings and danger, but it is also a color of passion (think of the heart and the blood that pumps through our veins). This person needs something to enthuse them. From the other ribbons drawn, it would seem that they have been through a difficult time. Might their spirit profit from doing something that excites them and connects them with the world again?

Other Ways of Reading Color

Ribbon reading is just one way of working with color but there are many others. Some may prefer to cast colored buttons in a fashion similar to rune or crystal reading, obtaining information from their color, shade, and size.

A pendulum is another way of gaining insight. For this you need a color wheel and a pendulum. Dangle the pendulum over the center of a color wheel and consider the question you want an answer for. As soon as you relax, the pendulum will begin to swing, pulling your attention toward one segment on the color chart. It might feel as though the pendulum has gained extra weight and is gravitating toward one specific color. Allow it to do so.

Read the color intuitively. Use what you know about its general meanings, but also make use of the way you feel about it. Darker colors will feel different than lighter ones, so yellow may provide a more favorable outcome than deep purple. Your intuition is your greatest ally, so allow yourself to trust the messages it provides. This will become easier with practice. If the pendulum doesn't choose a color that answers your question in full, relax and bring it back to the center of the wheel. Allowing it to pick a second color will add another layer to the message and provide greater understanding.

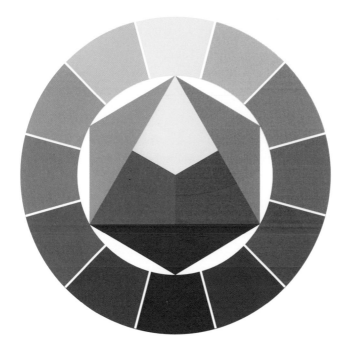

Colors and the Chakras

The chakras are seven energy points within the body, starting at the bottom of the torso and finishing at the top of the head. The system originated between 1500 and 500 BCE in India, first appearing in the Hindu Vedas. It is still immensely popular today and is a common component of yoga practice, and it can be an effective system of meaning in color readings. The chakras, meaning "wheel" or "turning," are stimulated to affect the well-being of a person. If they are blocked, they can be cleared through different forms of energy healing, such as reiki, meditation, or by using crystals. One possible way of reading color is to associate colors with their meanings in the chakra system.

First Chakra: Base or Root
Color: red
Position: base of the spine
Main roles: foundation, security, stability, safety
Issues when blocked: insecurity, scattered energy, worry, fear

Second Chakra: Sacral
Color: orange
Position: below the navel
Main roles: sexual health and energy, creativity
Issues when blocked: sexual problems, guilt, blocked creativity

Third Chakra: Solar Plexus
Color: yellow
Position: mid-torso, below chest
Main roles: power, personal responsibility
Issues when blocked: powerlessness, victim mentality, manipulation, lack of confidence

Fourth Chakra: Heart

Color: green
Position: chest
Main roles: relationships, love, self-love, feeling loved
Issues when blocked: problems in love, lack of self-love and respect, emotional difficulties

Fifth Chakra: Throat

Color: blue
Position: center of the neck
Main roles: communication, clear speech, making oneself heard
Issues when blocked: anxiety, feeling self-conscious, shyness, communication problems

Sixth Chakra: Third Eye

Color: indigo
Position: center of the brow
Main roles: vision, psychic abilities, intuition, foresight
Issues when blocked: lack of clarity, blocked intuition, illusion

Seventh Chakra: Crown

Color: purple
Position: top of the head
Main roles: connection with the divine, spiritual connection
Issues when blocked: disconnection from the spirit and higher consciousness

❋ ❋ ❋

9

READING
BUTTONS

One of the purposes of this book is to give the reader a variety of different divination methods that can be practiced at home without having to spend a lot of money. Like many of the tools described here, buttons are widely available and most people have some around the house or can acquire a small selection from a friend or for next to nothing from a thrift store.

The Tools That You Need

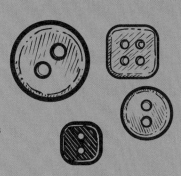

- A pretty cloth to put on a table or tray that you will throw your buttons on
- One white button and one black button, which will become *marker* buttons
- Nine more buttons of any other color or colors
- A clean mug

Method

Think about a problem or situation that you have in your life while you put all the buttons into the mug and give them a shake, then hold the mug above the table and pour the buttons onto the cloth. Check to see if the majority have landed nearer the white marker button or the black marker button, and whether they have fallen "hollow-side up," which is with the side upward that you would normally see on garment, or "hump-side up," which means the back of the button landed face up.

Near the White Marker

If most of the buttons fall near the white marker button, and most of them land with the hollow-side up, this is a fortunate omen: *You can expect health, wealth, and happiness over a prolonged period. All the following have promise if you give them due attention: love, business, and friendship.*

If the majority fall near the white marker, and most of them land with the hump-side, this is a fairly good omen: *There will be temporary setbacks and a halt to your happiness, but you can overcome these if you keep going. Look for new work, new opening for business, and new friends if necessary. Don't let your self-confidence be knocked, and you will win out in the end.*

Near the Black Marker

If the majority fall near the black marker button, and most of them land with the hollow-side up, this is a fairly good omen: *You are worrying unnecessarily, because while you do have problems, they are not large or important, so look for a rainbow. The truth is that unexpected good fortune will soon be on its way.*

If the majority fall near the black marker button, but with the hump-side up, the outlook is poor: *This is not a good omen for your job, career, or business, and it may be best to admit failure and bring something to an end rather than keep hoping that it will turn out all right in the end. If matters of love or friendship are mixed up in the situation, it could be a real disaster unless you identify the cause of the losses and bring them to an end.*

A Cross

If several of the buttons form themselves into a cross or an X, check out the following interpretations.

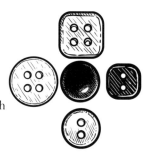

The buttons form a cross near the white marker, with most of the buttons hollow-side up: *Problems will spoil your happiness, but it is hard to say how bad this will be or how long it will go on for.*

The buttons form a cross near the white marker, with most of the buttons hump-side up: *You seem to be on the brink of doing something you will regret, so stop, think, and change direction if possible. If you have already done something regrettable or something that has hurt someone you care about, do what you can to put it right—if you can.*

The buttons form a cross near the black marker, with most of the buttons hollow-side up: *Some measure of good luck is due to come your way, and it won't be long before it does so.*

The buttons form a cross near the black marker, with most of the buttons hump-side up: *Luck may come your way, but something else may happen that spoils things for you, so don't take anything for granted.*

A Circle

If five or more buttons form a
circle, check out the following
interpretations:

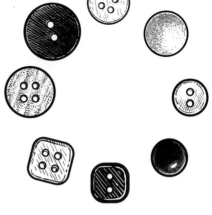

The buttons form a circle near the
white marker, with most of the
buttons hollow-side up: *Someone will
soon give you a valuable present, or you
will receive a nice sum of money.*

The buttons form a circle near the
white marker, with most of the
buttons hump-side up: *You will shortly take a pleasant journey, for business or
pleasure, and you can expect welcome visitors to your home.*

The buttons form a circle near the black marker, with most of the buttons
hollow-side up: *Something you are counting on will be disappointing or not worth the
effort.*

The buttons form a circle near the black marker, with most of the buttons
hump-side up: *A trip will be a waste of time at best, or it might be totally unprofitable
or even frighteningly dangerous. You are advised to forget travel for the next six
months at least.*

Four of Each

If eight of the buttons fall near one of the markers and four are hollow-side up
and four are hump-side up, you need to give your question some thought and
even ditch it and find another question to ask, then start the process again.

10

READING TEA LEAVES

In this book, we have looked at many human-made instruments for divination, but there is much to be found on our doorsteps. What we discover is often particular to where we live, but even within the cities and suburbs, the possibility of divining from nature exists within fallen feathers, flowers, and the sky above. Each is an example of a way in which our ancestors divined long before today's popular choices came into existence. Our own hands can be a tool for divination, as can the tea we drink.

Tasseography

Tasseography (also called tasseomancy) is the name given to using tea leaves to read one's fortune. Originating from the Arabic word *tassa* (meaning "cup") and the Greek word *mancy* (meaning "divination"), the art of tea leaf reading gained popularity in the seventeenth century when tea was introduced into Europe from China.

Drinking tea with friends is an enjoyable pastime, and it could just be that people began to see the topics of their conversations appearing in the shapes of the leaves left in their cups after a get-together. As this form of divination gained greater interest, people would gather for a hot cup of tea with the express purpose of having their fortunes told once they'd finished drinking. As with playing-card divination, the teacup was yet another way in which diviners could practice in plain sight without interference or judgment.

Tasseography is still a popular method of divining the future, and you can buy cups designed for the purpose. These cups have designated areas to read if a leaf falls on them, but a cup like this is not necessary. In fact, the more uncluttered the cup, the better it is for reading.

Choosing Your Cup

• A dark or colored cup will make reading the tea leaves difficult, as it makes it harder to see symbols. It's best to use a white cup, as it will help you to see the patterns clearly.

- It is best that your cup has no patterning on the inside. Patterns, however small, can obstruct symbols, making it difficult to read them.
- A proper teacup with a wide brim is best, because if you use a mug or other cup that is tall and narrow, the leaves will not stick to the sides as easily. Readers take the location of leaves into consideration, including their depth in the cup, so a wider cup will make this process easier.
- You will also need a saucer, so pick a cup-and-saucer set if you can. It is not strictly necessary, since a small plate can be used as a substitute. It is important that the handle does not rise above the top rim of the cup. Otherwise, this would prevent the cup from sitting flush with the saucer when it is tipped upside down.

Choosing Your Tea

- Black tea is preferable for tea leaf reading, since darker tea can be easily seen in the cup. It also sinks to the bottom, which makes the process of drinking the unstrained tea more enjoyable.
- Old fashioned tea that has longish leaves and which is uniform in shape can make for better readings since it will naturally build more interesting shapes.
- Opening a tea bag does not really work. The tea inside is too fine and dusty, which makes it unpleasant to drink and hard to read.
- Different teas can be used for different kinds of readings. Rose tea, as an example, can be used for love readings, and nettle might be an apt choice if protection or personal power is required. However, general black tea is good for all kinds of questions.

Setting Up Your Tea and Reading Space

As with any type of divination, it is important to set your intention and work in an organized and clean space (see pages 8–9 in the introduction for more on this). If you are using a teapot, a few teaspoons of tea will be enough, but remember that it is important to use a pot that does not have a built-in strainer at the base of the spout. Alternatively, most people just place a few pinches of tea into a cup and then pour boiling water over it. It is at this point, while the tea steeps, that you consider your question or area of interest.

Directions for Tea Leaf Reading

Let your tea steep for a few minutes.

Drink your tea, thinking about the subject you want to know about, but remember to leave about a teaspoon of the liquid in the cup. This will help the leaves to move about when the cup is turned.

Place the saucer over the top of the cup carefully, making sure that the handle is facing you, then turn the cup upside down onto the saucer. Some people like to hold their hands over the cup for a few seconds and actually ask the question or state their intention.

Turn the cup around on the saucer three times in a counterclockwise direction. This will allow the leaves to move about the cup and for some to fall away. Make sure that the handle is directed toward you at the end of each turn. Leave the cup on the saucer for a few minutes once finished.

It is now time to turn the cup upright with the handle still facing you. Before doing so, some readers like to tap the bottom of the cup three times with their nondominant hand.

It is now time to assess the symbols you find within the cup. This takes practice, so don't expect to master this on your first go. There might only be a few images that strike you. Go with what you see and trust your intuition. Tea leaf reading is personal to each reader. If you see only a couple of symbols, then these are what is important at this time.

There are common interpretations of the symbols, but your own feelings about what they mean are just as relevant. An animal could refer to its characteristics (such as cunning for a fox or the view seen by that of a flying bird) but some could relate to your pets too. Use your gut feelings to read the symbols and to assess what they might mean in your life.

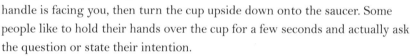

Examine dots and lines and look for figures. Some clusters of leaves might resemble letters.

Symbol Placements

The way you choose to read is up to you, so experiment until you find a way that you are comfortable with and then stay consistent in your reading method.

The placement of the leaves within your cup is important. Most readers use the depth of the cup for readings, which is why a wider bowl-like shape is preferable to a tall mug. It makes the symbols easier to see.

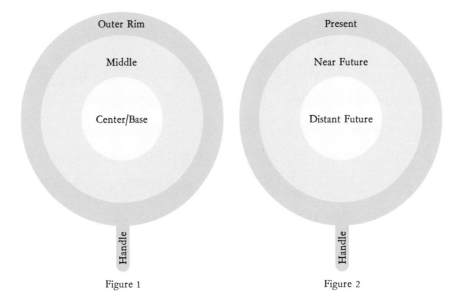

Figure 1   Figure 2

Many people want to know what is going on in the present and what to prepare for. For this reason, the cup can be sectioned out in the following way.

Any symbols that sit around the rim talk about things that are likely to happen soon or are happening in the present. These could reflect the nature of the question or fears of the questioner. The farther toward the base the leaves fall, the further into the future they go. Symbols that appear in the center will reflect those things likely to happen as things stand in your life at the moment. Remember that you are in charge of your destiny, so if you do not like what you see, now is the time to make steps toward changing it.

Notice how the leaves have dispersed. If there are larger clumps or if they gravitate to specific areas of the cup, it could mean that there will be more going on in that time frame. Some readers prefer to read the sections as past, present, and future, with the past sitting at the base and the rim as the future.

Dividing the Cup into Quarters

Another method for reading into the future is to divide the cup into quarters, with each representing a different period of time. This is why it helps to have the handle facing you, so that the different areas can be determined.

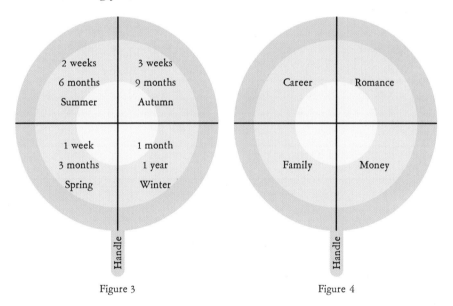

Figure 3   Figure 4

As you can see from the illustration, there are many ways in which time can be interpreted. The four sections correspond nicely to either a month of time (four weeks) or a season. Depending on where you are in your year, the first section, at the bottom left, can denote the season you are in. For example, if you are in June, then the first quarter will signify summer and so on.

These labels can be altered to suit the reading and reader. For a life reading, they might be changed to childhood, adolescence, midlife, and old age, but they can also depict areas of interest too, as shown in the example above.

The Symbols

Reading the symbols is a personal art, and you must not forget that your reaction to them is relevant. For the beginner, however, the following list may be of some help since it shows common interpretations of symbols, some modern and others handed down over time.

Symbol	Meaning
Airplane	Journey, vacation
Anchor	Stability, lack of movement
Angel	Good news, messages from the angels
Ant	Teamwork, industry
Apple	Knowledge, desire to learn
Arrow	Difficult news (look to where it is pointing)
Baby	Birth, new beginnings, new arrival
Ball	Fluctuation, the ups and downs of life
Balloon	Things are improving, looking up
Bat	Warning, secret enemies
Bear	Dangerous environment, beware
Bee	Effort, discipline
Bell	Good fortune, revelation

Symbol	Meaning
Bird	Good news, messages
Boat	Sea travel, a cruise, a trip; if upside down, dangers and problems with trust
Book	Information, knowledge, education
Boot	Protection, standing up for yourself
Bouquet	Gifts, compliments, good omen
Bracelet	Unions, partnerships, bonds
Bridge	Shortcut, opportunities for success
Butterfly	Enjoyable pursuits, social time
Cage	Restriction, frustration
Cake	Celebration, gatherings, parties
Candle	Philanthropic gestures
Castle	High society, official business, ego
Cat	Suspicion, unsuspected enemy, hidden motives
Chain	Relationships (note if it is intact or broken)
Circle	Completion, finalization, the end of a phase
Clock	Time is running out and is of the essence

Symbol	Meaning
Clouds	Unhappiness, depression, doubt
Coffin	Endings, illness
Coin	Money, financial opportunity
Comma	Pause in life
Cross	Suffering, sacrifice
Crown	Authority
Cup	Reward
Dagger	Treachery, enemy
Dog	Loyalty, faithfulness
Dove	Peace, happiness
Dragon	Terror, fear
Duck	Wealth, financial gain
Eagle	Leadership, power, influence
Ear	Gossip, scandal, rumors
Egg	Fresh start, new projects
Elephant	Wise soul, sagacity, moral strength
Eye	Perception, supervision, details

Symbol	Meaning
Fairy	Romance, adventure, fun
Fan	Flirtation, concealment of truth
Feather	Instability
Fire	Anger, disruption
Fish	Successful endeavors, plenty, money, good omen
Flower	Small wishes granted
Fly	Minor domestic problems
Foot	Discretion, wisdom
Fork	Decisions to be made, choice
Fox	Betrayal, cunning, treachery, untruths
Frog	Self-importance, pride
Grapes	Prosperity, material pleasures
Gun	Attack, hurtful gossip
Hand	New friendship, success, social matters
Hare	Timidity, fear
Hat	New interests
Heart	Love, affection (near a ring, marriage is suggested)

Symbol	Meaning
Helmet	Trust
Hill	Obstacle
Horse	Wisdom, service to others, charity
Horseshoe	Good luck, pleasant omen, fortune
House	Safety, security
Ivy	Faithfulness, reliability, assistance
Jester	Frivolity, foolishness
Key	Solutions, success
Knife	Separation, cutting something away
Ladder	Advancement, initiative, labor
Lantern	Guidance, protection
Leaf	News
Leg	Activity, movement
Letter	Mail, correspondence
Lion	Authority, honor, greatness
Mask	Deception, secrets

Symbol	Meaning
Mermaid	Temptation, seduction
Monkey	Mischief, monkeying around, playful person
Moon	A full moon denotes a love affair. A crescent moon suggests new projects, whereas a waxing moon signifies difficulties within general affairs.
Mountain	Ambition, goals, obstacles to be overcome
Mouse	Poverty, hard times
Mushroom	Expansion, sudden growth
Numbers	Relevant dates or indicators of time—days, weeks, months, years
Oak Tree	Long life, good health
Owl	Difficult omen, regarding business and well-being
Palm Tree	Honors, victory
Parrot	Gossip, tattletale
Peacock	Vanity
Pear	Ease, comfort
Pentagon	Intelligence, mental strength, focus
Pig	Warning against greed or indulgence

Symbol	Meaning
Rabbit	Timidity, sensitivity, lack of confidence, fertility
Rainbow	Hope, belief in better times, dreams
Rat	Do not underestimate others, opponent
Ring	Commitment, bond, proposal
Road	A new path awaits
Rose	True friendship, unconditional love
Scales	Justice, fairness, legal issues
Scissors	Bickering, arguments
Shark	Danger lurks, unkindness
Sheep	Docility, a follower, a need to stand up for oneself
Ship	Prosperity
Skull	Danger, warning, don't take unnecessary risks
Snake	Mistrust, an enemy
Spider	Persistence, hard work, effort
Spiral	A slow advancement
Square	Feeling restricted, blocked

Symbol	Meaning
Star	Good fortune, accomplishment of dreams
Sun	Warmth, vitality, happiness, power
Swan	Grace, contentment
Sword	Disputes, challenges
Table	Social get-togethers, feasts
Tent	Feeling unsettled, not committed
Tortoise	Slow, sensitive, withdrawal
Triangle	If pointing upward, success; if pointing downward, disappointment and difficulty
Umbrella	Protection, shelter
Vase	Usefulness to others, being of service
Violin	Independence, walking your own path, individuality
Volcano	Holding things in is not healthy, suppressing something
Wasp	Hurt feelings, pain
Wheel	Advancement, fortune, going with the flow
Zebra	Long journey

❋ ❋ ❋

11

READING FLOWERS

It is possible to read fortunes with any of nature's tools, and flowers, in all their varieties, are no exception. In fact, there are many systems of floromancy (the term used for divination through flowers) in use, ranging from the traditional to the modern. Most diviners today will combine the handed-down meanings of the flowers and their own intuition when reading a single flower and its parts.

It is generally accepted, well outside the realm of divination, that most flowers have meanings. Some, like the rose, are more obvious, though different colors of the same variety will provoke different responses and, therefore, different interpretations. The red rose, famously linked to love and romance, has a different connotation than its yellow sister, which is a symbol of friendship.

Flowers are often given and used with reference to their meanings rather than how they look. For example, the lily is considered a funeral flower. While its white coloring was thought to mean purity and innocence by the ancient Greeks and Romans, the Stargazer lily is a symbol of sympathy for many. In the Victorian era, interest in flowers grew considerably, and they were often passed between people as a way of communicating secrets that they felt couldn't be spoken aloud. Directories of meanings were compiled for interpretation, including *Le langage des fleurs*, written by Louise Cortambert and published in 1819 under the pen name of Madame Charlotte de Latour. This means of communication through flowers is known as floriography.

Flower Meanings

There have been many books and articles written about how to use flowers in healing practices, and these concentrate on how a flower can be used in a remedy rather than its traditional meaning. If you take the aforementioned Stargazer as an example, it is viewed quite differently by healers, who will use it to encourage security and self-worth.

There have been many meanings attributed to flowers over the centuries, so it is likely that some variations will exist contrary to those given here, which are in line with symbolism used in the 1800s.

Flower	Meaning
Begonia	Warning, dark thoughts, caution needed
Belladonna	Silence
Bluebell	Humility, gratitude
Buttercup	Childish behavior, immaturity
Camellia	Affection, longing
Carnation (White)	Purity in love, good luck for women
Carnation (Yellow)	Disdain, rejection, disappointment
Daffodil	Rebirth, new beginnings
Daisy	Innocence, hope
Forget-me-not	Memories
Gardenia	Secret love
Geranium	Friendship
Hyacinth	Play
Iris	Messages, communications, faith
Lavender	Distrust
Lily (Calla)	Beauty
Lily (Stargazer)	Sympathy
Lotus	Enlightenment
Marigold	Grief, jealousy
Petunia	Resentment, anger

Flower	Meaning
Poppy	Consolation
Rose (pink)	Happiness
Rose (red)	Love, romance
Rose (yellow)	Friendship
Sunflower	Long life, loyalty, longevity
Tulip (red)	Passion
Violet	Devotion

Reading a Flower

It is common for a floromancer to select a handful of different flowers and either lay them out or put them in a small vase for the questioner to choose from. The person being read for must be guided by their own intuition when selecting a flower from those available. This is one area of divination where consciously choosing something will aid the reading, as the questioner will be drawn to a specific flower for a reason, and that will tell the reader something about the hidden motivations of the questioner. If you wish to read for yourself, you might wish to place the flowers in a pot, lightly turning it to mix them, and pull one with your eyes closed.

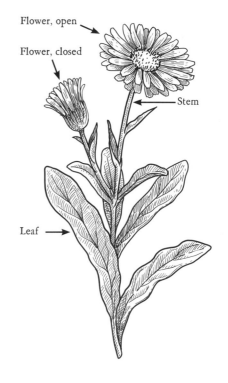

Flower, open

Flower, closed

Stem

Leaf →

Different parts of a flower will relate to different areas of a person's life, and what you feel as you gently run your finger over the flower is as important as what you see. The following guide should inspire your flower-reading technique.

Stem

The stem is considered to account for a person's past. The length is important, since the nearer you get to your flower, the nearer to the present time you are. Check for any lumps or bumps and notice whether it feels smooth. A smooth stem will indicate a happier past or a happy childhood, while irregularities or discoloration will relay challenges or periods of unhappiness or distress. A weak stem can suggest the fragility of a person and show either sensitivity or a lack of confidence.

> **Tip**
>
> •••••◆◆◆◆•••••
>
> Note that some flowers, such as daffodils and tulips, have entirely smooth stems and may not be useful for this purpose.

Should there be any small buds or leaves on your stem, secondary to the main flower, these will suggest life-changing diversions, or they could indicate children of one's own or other children who the querent cares for, or maybe significant past relationships.

Flower

The flower represents the present, and a lot can be detected by how it appears. If it is closed, opportunities and new beginnings are suggested, but there may be a delay in something coming to fruition.

When a flower is open, you can read the different areas as you look at it from above. The outer leaves will provide messages about the physical body, the inner ring of leaves relate to the emotional life, and the stamen, in the center, speaks of the individual's spiritual core. Note what condition the petals are in. Any tears, tatters, or missing spaces all have relevance, as do changes in color. Allow your intuition to take the lead and trust what you feel.

The flower as a whole has something to say too. Vibrant flowers will describe larger-than-life personalities or big dreams, whereas small flowers indicate someone who prefers a quiet life or who wants to be closer to home and family.

Flower Scrying

Flower scrying can be performed in a variety of ways, but an ancient method, used by the Romans, has the diviner scattering petals and dried flowers into water. Not unlike the traditional method of tea leaf reading, the diviner will become aware of certain shapes and the placement of the flowers.

This process can be practiced in any small vessel of water, but it is better to use a sizable bowl with a diameter of at least 12 inches (30 centimeters). This will give the flower pieces enough space to flow and then settle, forming a good basis for a reading.

Any kinds of flowers can be used for this divination, but it will work best if they are either small or if you use just parts of the flower, such as the petals, leaves, and pieces of stems. Multiple species can be used, or if you wish your reading to be themed, those that are associated with what is on the questioner's mind (see the flower definitions above). Having an assortment of different flowers and colors is desirable if you wish them to ignite your intuition.

Fill the bowl with water almost to the top. Any water will work, but if you wish to use water from a natural source, such as a pond, you can. This is

down to preference, and if you wish to bless your bowl of water beforehand
or say some kind of prayer, it will add to the spirit of what you are doing and
strengthen your intention. Ritual is not absolutely necessary, but it can be an
effective way of getting ready for the work you are about to do. A few words,
from the heart, are often enough.

   With your nondominant hand, take a small handful of flowers or petals
and pieces and scatter them onto the surface of the water. Then gently stir the
water with your fingers, keeping your question in mind or saying it aloud. Once
you feel you have done this enough, sit back and allow the flowers to find their

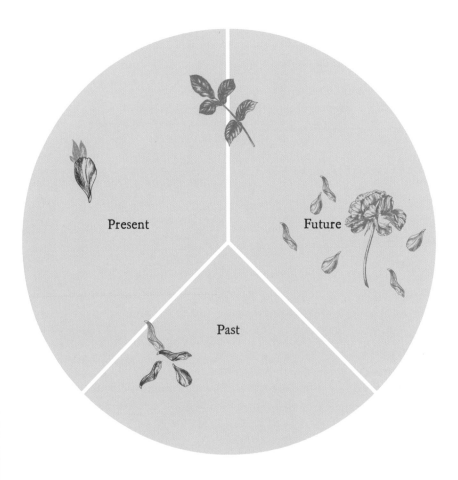

resting places. Once they have settled, you are ready to begin your reading. You can now evaluate where the flowers are and what you feel they are telling you.

Do you notice any significant groupings? Perhaps four petals have fallen in a cluster. Could the number four have meaning that is associated with the question?

How do the flowers sit together? Do they suggest recognizable shapes which might be relevant or have personal meaning? Do some of the flowers overlap? What might that mean in the context of your reading? A red petal overlapping a blue one could suggest that passion or sexual energy (red) has a dominant edge in a romantic reading.

You may wish to separate your bowl into thirds, assigning each to a different time frame—perhaps past, present, and future such as in the example provided.

In the example on the previous page, we can see that darker petals sit within the person's past, potentially speaking of a difficult period. There are three of them, which could signify a three-year-long relationship or something that happened three years ago. The pink petal moves into the present, suggesting that there is a need to move on from this, though a past situation still has a hold over the person.

The two petals in the present look like a person wearing a crown. Might this present a need for taking control and finding authority? Taking responsibility could be part of the message here.

The stem crosses over from the present to the future. Like a bridge, it could suggest an opportunity or helping hand.

If this reading concerns a person's love life, then the pink flower at the end could indicate a new romantic relationship. Being the only full flower in the reading, this could speak of a wholesome and satisfying union. The small petals that surround it could convey much happiness (the many petals meaning an abundance) or may even appear as confetti for the reader, suggesting marriage.

✳ ✳ ✳

12

READING
SHELLS

Conchomancy, which is pronounced *conko-mancy*, is a form of divination that uses seashells. The ocean is of great fascination to many, due to its beauty and mystery. While it can be calm and healing, it can also become chaotic, dark, and immensely powerful. In Greek mythology, it was the home of many fantastical creatures, and it was ruled over by Poseidon, the god of the sea. There have been many stories of helpful and manipulative sea nymphs, and most of us are aware of the captivating beauty and seductive powers of the mermaid in fantasy fiction.

For the diviner, the beach is a treasure trove of tools. There is often a rich tapestry of pebbles, each with their own shapes, markings, and character, and among them can be found shells of different varieties and sizes, like diamonds in the rough. A seashell is the protective outer later created by some animals that live in the sea. It is the exoskeleton of an invertebrate, and if you find it on the beach, it has likely died and been consumed by another animal. This outer shell was once its protection and security; in short, its home.

One of the bonuses of working with our natural environment—the earth, ocean, and sky—is that it comes with its own energy, and we can interpret it in ways that feel right to each of us. Nature's creations are not human made. Often, the oracle tools that we find in our gardens, on our walks, or by beach-combing have already been immersed in life itself, whether they be sea-covered shells or the feathers of a bird. We accept these gifts from Mother Nature and can easily include them into our magical practice if we so wish.

Seashells are used for divination all around the world, though using cowrie shells for readings is possibly the best known. This practice comes from West Africa and is used within the Santería, Umbanda, and Candomblé religions. Many practitioners will use this style of shell and its unique markings and shape to make predictions about the future or help provide guidance in the present.

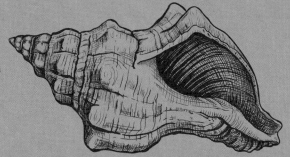

How to Choose Shells

The best way to build a collection of shells is to walk along the beach and find them for yourself, though there are other ways of collecting them for your work. Sets can be bought online easily, and there are shops that will sell individual shells. Buying, rather than finding, can mean a greater variety, and you'll locate some shells that you'd be unlikely to see on your local beach, if you live near one. If you choose to find your own, though, allow the ocean to guide your exploration, and don't forget to thank her for the gifts you take home with you.

It is important that you feel a connection to the shells that you choose. Let your intuition guide what you see and what you feel. Not every shell needs to be perfect or a myriad of colors. Each will have its own beauty and meaning. Broken shells or fragments of shells have as much value as those that are still whole. Consider the size of what you find and how easy it will be to use as an oracle. Those that are too large might not be as easy to use as those that can be comfortably held in your hand, so perhaps a piece of a typically large shell is better to use than the whole thing.

The Shapes and Styles of Shells

There are far too many types of shells to mention in this book, but all can be used for divination if you consider their shape and markings. The following are examples of common shell styles as well as descriptions of how you might begin to read those shells.

Abalone

The abalone has an oval shape, and its coloring is
significant. All of the colors of the sea are found
within its silvery inner surface, though the outside
of the shell is dull in comparison. Known as the "ear
of the sea," the abalone is connected to love, peace,

compassion, and emotional issues. While it may resemble a shield to some,
it is associated with healing for many. If this shell turns up in a reading, then
an emotional issue may be significant, but it could also suggest that love and
affection are in the air. Make note of which way it falls, since the dull side
could suggest a lack of these qualities or a need for peace, resolution, or
companionship.

Clam

Clamshells are hinged and thus called bivalves. Some
have a scallop shape, but there are smooth ones as well
as ones that have a wavy edge.

 If we think about the definition of the word *clam*
and the purpose of the shell, we understand that something is hidden within.
We often think of someone who holds something back out of fear, as in
clamming up, for example. They may lack in confidence or feel withdrawn. With
this in mind, this shape (if both parts are drawn) could suggest secrets or even
the inability to socialize or speak out. When this shell arrives in a reading, you
might need to consider what is being held back.

Conch

The robust conch has been referred to as a
"seashell horn" or "shell trumpet," because when
you blow through it, it makes a trumpeting
sound. For this reason, it has been used to call
attention in important events or celebrations.
With this in mind, the shape can be easily associated with communication
or announcements of all kinds, making it a shell that signifies news or
messages of importance in a reading.

Cone

A cone-shaped shell has sections, and its height is gradual rather than severe. Reminiscent of a coned turret on a castle, it could suggest security but also authority. For some practitioners, the shape of this shell symbolizes stability and the home life, whereas others might see it as a crown and link it to power and dominion.

Cowrie

The cowrie shell has an egglike shape. Aside from its distinctive patterning, it can be recognized by the small row of teeth on its belly. The shape is reminiscent of a woman's sexual organs and, therefore, can be associated

with fertility and passion. As a lucky charm, the shell is also connected to wealth and good fortune. Think about how the cowrie feels in your hand; it is smooth on one side but the teeth beneath are in contrast to its back. What does this tell you? Might it remind you to guard yourself? Are those protruding teeth protecting something inside that is vulnerable?

Keyhole

The keyhole shell is conical in shape but low, usually with an indent at its tip. While the shape of this shell will be of interest to the diviner, it is the hole that is probably most significant. What would a hole symbolize for you?

Might you see it as something missing in life, or could it represent a doorway or opportunity, or something to be hoped for or feared? This could have an impact on how you feel about moving on to a new phase in life.

Scallop

The scallop is well-known for being the shape of shell that carried Venus to shore in the painting *The Birth of Venus* by Sandro Botticelli. This, in itself, could suggest new beginnings and births of all kinds, but the shape of the shell may also bring growth and creativity to the fore, since it unfolds from a point like a fan.

It is important to note the lines on the outer side of the shell because they could represent many paths. When upside down, they all lead to one point, potentially meaning focus. When the base is at the bottom, the paths represent scattered energies or a lack of direction.

Nautilus

The nautilus shape contains a large spiral on one side. This shell, like that of a snail, could indicate things taking time, since the spiral appears to go on indefinitely. When alive, the nautilus shell continues to grow and house the animal. Therefore, the meaning for this shell could include expansion. The  more we learn in life, the more we grow and develop. This shell may concern the accumulation of knowledge or our outgrowing of a situation or relationship. Like the nautilus, any mollusk that continues to grow could represent change in your readings.

Spiked

Some shells will be irregular in shape and contain spikes. While these will not be dangerous for you to hold, they could symbolize a warning in a reading. A spiked shell might suggest caution or someone out to cause trouble or who, at best, is prickly. If a prominent spike points toward another shell in a casting, it could alert the reader to an area of their life where vigilance is needed.

Starfish

The starfish is not strictly a shell, but you may well come across them in all sizes, from the large to the mini. This sea creature is related to the stars in the sky and is therefore attributed similar correspondences to the Star card in tarot, which talks of guidance and hope during difficult times. Generally, this celestial symbol can provide inspiration in a reading.

Tower Shell

The tower shell is easy to recognize, since it is tall and slender with up to twenty windings. Unlike the nautilus, which also has a spiral shape, the emphasis here is on height. The silhouette of the shell could bring masculinity and the male sex organ to mind, which could have particular relevance in a reading connected to drive or dominance, though it may also suggest perception. It is when we rise above a situation that we can see it for what it really is.

Reading with Shells

How a diviner uses shells is personal to them. Some will cast on a cloth or draw from a bag randomly. When reading for another person, however, there are those who will lay the shells out and ask the questioner to pick those that they are drawn to. The methods for casting runes can easily apply to shells, though it is worth reflecting on which shells land faceup or facedown. Some readers will ignore inverted objects in other forms of divination, but with shells, there is as much to be gained from the underside of some as there is from the outer surface.

What to Look for in Your Shell

Even though the shape and style of the shell are relevant in reading, there are other significant factors to look out for.

- How does your shell feel? Is it smooth or does it have a harsh exterior? Sometimes, appearances can be deceiving, and if your intuition is drawn to the texture of your shell, it could add an extra layer to your interpretation. Rougher layers could suggest obstacles or challenges, whereas smoother surfaces might bring easier solutions to problems.
- What pattern is on your shell? Does it have spots or stripes? Is the pattern more intense in one part than another? Think about how this could answer your question.

• What is the color of your shell? Is it
bright or dull? Do you feel uplifted or
dispirited when you view it?

• Is your shell complete or broken?
If the shell is broken or chipped, this
could have relevance within a reading. If more
than one of the same type of shell is cast but
if only one has a chip, it could suggest that
something is damaged and irreparable, but this
experience is giving the questioner strength
and experience.

• If your shell has spikes, how many are there?
Might these correspond to days, months,
or years?

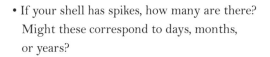

• Does your shell have any growths on it? Some
will have tiny barnacles or even pieces of
seaweed or discoloration. All of these features
are worthy of reading. Determine what an add-
on could symbolize with regards to the subject
of your reading.

• Listen to your shell. Hold it up to your ear to see if you can hear
anything worth noting.

❊ ❊ ❊

13

THE
I CHING

The *I Ching* (pronounced "eee ching," "yee ching," or "ee jing") is known as the *Book of Changes*, but the translation would actually be better expressed as *A Scroll of Good Advice Concerning How to Deal with Calamity and Disaster*. It is also the name used for the system of divination described in the book.

The origins of parts of the *I Ching* are thought to go back 7,000 years or more, but in those early days, knowledge was passed on by word of mouth, so no written records survive. The early *I Ching* may have stemmed from a series of parables, but the original thinking behind the system has been lost over time. Much of the *I Ching* that we use today was researched and written by King Wen and further developed by his son, the Duke of Zhou, who wrote the individual lines of the hexagrams around 1027 BCE. As with many of the tools that have remained useful over a long period of time, some of the meanings have become outdated and sexist. It is important to remember this when reading the hexagrams and, in some cases, be flexible with their meanings. Sensitivity is always recommended when reading for others.

The Hexagrams

When you work with the hexagrams (the shapes created when you throw the coins in the I Ching system), you will notice that they don't go into details about love and relationships, although the items are mentioned in passing, so to speak. It seems that the ancient Chinese were preoccupied with their farms, families, and becoming prosperous enough to survive hard times rather than worrying about their love lives.

Coins

The most popular method of working out the I Ching these days is to use three coins. You can buy special Chinese coins, but there is no need, because you can use ordinary coins so long as they are all the same denomination. Give your coins a good wash and dry them using a paper towel. Then hold them in your hand and ask the universe to bless them. It would be worth keeping them in a safe place after use, so they are ready for you to use again in the future.

Tip

You will need a pen and paper to read the I Ching. You will also need a tray or a table with a clean cloth on it.

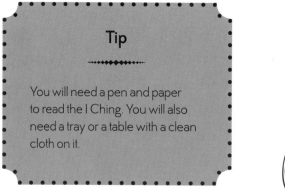

Throwing the Coins

Think of something that is on your mind and pick up your three coins. Shake them in your hand for a moment and then throw them down gently onto your tray or table. If the majority of coins fall with their heads up, draw an unbroken line on your piece of paper. This is a *yang* line. If all three coins fell heads up, mark a small cross at the end of the line. This will be a changing line, and I will come back to those later in this chapter.

─────────────────

An unbroken line from a majority of heads

──────────────✕

An unbroken line from three heads (this is a changing line)

If the majority of your coins fell tails up, draw a line with a break in it. This is a *yin* line. If all three coins fall with their tails up, mark the end of the line with a small cross to indicate a changing line.

Throw the coins again and draw a second line *above* the previous one.

A broken line from a majority of tails

A broken line from three tails (this is a changing line)

Repeat this four more times for four lines, each one above the other, until you have six lines. This is your hexagram.

A hexagram with two broken lines and two changing lines

Interpreting the Hexagrams

1. Ch'ien
CREATIVITY, THE KING

This hexagram is the most masculine, paternal, and muscular of the hexagrams, so it shows that you will need to act with courage and confidence, to focus on your goals and go all out for what you want. Initiate new ideas and use your energy wisely. In business you need to show leadership and authority, while your loved ones will turn to you for direction. Use your strength wisely and don't be aggressive or obstinate. This powerful hexagram refers to the opening of an important new phase in your life.

2. K'un
RECEPTIVITY, THE QUEEN

This is the most motherly and feminine of the hexagrams. You will have to adjust to circumstances and not make waves. To some extent, your future happiness is in the hands of others, so fit in with their desires and don't just think of yourself. This powerful hexagram emphasizes the bygone feminine virtues of endurance, duty, and patience. Go with the flow for a while and use your intuition.

3. Chun
DIFFICULTY AT THE START

You are at the beginning of a new phase and don't know
where this will lead. You must break new ground, and while
nothing will happen quickly, it will be successful. A new relationship might be
in the air.

4. Meng
YOUTH, FOLLY, INEXPERIENCE

You need to study or update skills, so you should take advice
and learn slowly. If you are misunderstood, explain yourself
to others. Don't put on airs and graces, but be ready to listen to wise words.
Treat others kindly and generously.

5. Hsu
WAITING

Don't plunge into anything, and if life is quiet at the
moment, take a rest, meditate for inner wisdom, and listen to
the advice of sincere friends. Ambition and advancement are on the way, even
if they are not evident just yet. It may be beneficial to cross water for business
or personal reasons.

6. Sung
CONFLICT

Accept criticism or put up with not receiving credit for your
work. Although you are probably in the right, this is not a
good time to argue or to state your point. If you need to ask for advice, consult
a wise person. Don't attempt large undertakings in business or elsewhere,
because maintaining a steady course is the best option. Love and marriage are
not favorable at the moment.

7. Shih
THE ARMY, COLLECTIVE FORCE, LEADERSHIP

A battle is ahead, and you need to maintain the confidence of
those who depend upon you. Others are on hand to help, and
spiritual guidance is also close by. You have to decide whether you should fight
against injustice or retreat from this particular skirmish.

8. Pi
UNION, JOINING

You need to join others in a collective campaign at work or
within the family, and you need to work for the benefit of
those around you as well as for yourself. This is a favorable time for trust in
business and for love relationships.

9. Hsiao Ch'u
TAMING SMALL POWERS, RESTRAINT

Times may be hard for a while, but a sensible and economic
approach is best, and you will appreciate the good times all
the more when they arrive. Practice restraint and sincerity, and consider others.
If a relationship isn't working, you may have to leave it.

10. Lu
TREADING, CAUTION

Leave things as they are until more favorable conditions
apply. Be firm, even with yourself, and tread the straight and
narrow path. Don't allow others to take advantage or force you to lose your
stride. Use intuition.

11. T'ai
PEACE, HARMONY, PROSPERITY

A time of peace, harmony, and happiness, but remember to
share some of your happiness and good fortune with those
who are less well-off. This is a time to plant crops for the future or to harvest
crops from the past.

12. P'i
STAGNATION, DISHARMONY

Poverty, losses, and hard times are around you, but a change
in outlook or attitude will help. Do not be discouraged,
because sometimes good things emerge out of misfortune. Be modest and don't
make a fuss, even though relationships are difficult right now.

13. T'ung Jen
FELLOWSHIP, COMMUNITY

Teamwork is the key to success, although you may need
to become the leader of the team. Competitors and battles
in business will occur, but you will soon make better progress and pass from
obscurity to a brighter and more successful future. Success is yours, but you
must share the benefits with others and work with colleagues if you can.

14. Ta Yu
GREAT POSSESSIONS, WEALTH

Riches, wealth, and success are assured. You will soon be
doing very well, but you may incur jealousy or small losses
due to allowing money matters to drift. Work and study will go together, and
you will soon be in a better position to understand the tasks ahead of you. Don't
try to impress others; just grasp the basics and get on with your job quietly.

15. Ch'ien
MODESTY, MODERATION

Avoid extremes and try to achieve a balance in your life. Be
modest but don't be stupidly humble or allow others to turn
you into a victim.

16. Yu
HAPPINESS, ENTHUSIASM

The meaning of this hexagram is *preparation* and having the
enthusiasm to set out on a new project. You must ensure that all
is in order and that there are no loose ends left hanging from previous situations
before you make a start. You will need to advertise yourself and your wares and
create an enthusiastic atmosphere, but don't get a big head in the process.

17. Sui
FOLLOWING, ADAPTING

This is a good time for marriage and personal life, but it isn't
a fortunate time for business affairs or friendship. In business
it would be best to drift with the current and allow others to show you the way
or take the initiative on your behalf. You will be in charge of your own affairs
again soon.

18. Ku
REPAIRING, CLEARING CLUTTER, REVISING

Losses, setbacks, and hardship abound, and in various areas of your life, trouble seems to be all around. A change of luck is on the way, but you need to put right something that is wrong, so you may have to apologize or correct a misunderstanding. Be scrupulously honest in all your dealings.

19. Lin
APPROACH, PROMOTION, GATHERING STRENGTH

You need to deal kindly with those who report to you. You will soon be in an excellent position yourself, so this is the time to be generous to others. Another interpretation tells us that a daughter should listen carefully to her mother and follow her advice. This hexagram also suggests that your luck will improve in the month of August.

20. Kuan
OBSERVATION, CONTEMPLATION, UNDERSTANDING

Now is the time to take up a course of study or to train for something new. It is also favorable to meditate and to go on an inward journey to analyze yourself. You will need to keep your eyes open for opportunities and contemplate wider issues. Don't take things on trust; look beyond what is obvious and use your intuition.

21. Shih Ho
CHEWING, REFORM, BITING THROUGH

Concentrate on the positive achievements that you have made, however small they may be, and refuse to allow others to stress the negative or unsuccessful aspects of your life. Don't let jealous people get you down. If someone is interfering in your love relationship, keep cool because they will soon lose their influence and peace will return to your household.

22. Pi
GRACEFULNESS, ORNAMENT

Dress nicely and look successful in order to sell an idea or give an appearance of success, but once you have accomplished your aim, don't continue to live beyond your means. There will

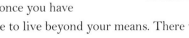

soon be extra expenses and fewer opportunities. Contemplation and solitude will bring equilibrium back into your life.

23. Po
DECAY, DISINTEGRATION

A man may have many girlfriends, but he can easily lose his money, looks, charisma—and eventually all the girlfriends as well! For women, this is a troublesome period when backstabbing and gossiping abound. Some aspect of your life will be destroyed, but you will soon be able to build afresh for the future. Guard against a situation where people who are close to you undermine you.

24. Fu
RETURN, TURNING POINT

Attune yourself to nature, to the seasons, and develop a sense of timing because a change of season will bring improvements and a renewal of energy. Be patient. Reunions are likely. Oddly enough, this hexagram is not favorable for matters relating to first marriages, but it is good for subsequent ones.

25. Wu Wang
INNOCENCE

Don't rush in where angels fear to tread. Be honest, stay within your own limitations, and allow heaven to guide you. Be unselfish and uncomplicated, and don't let temporary setbacks upset you. Take advice from your father or from a respected leader and good fortune will follow. An important undertaking is on the way.

26. Ta Ch'u
TAMING THE GREAT POWERS

This hexagram is like a bow string because it represents power that is stored up, which, when released, can go far. You will soon make great advances in your career, and hard work and steady progress will bring success. Difficulties will be overcome, and even difficult people can be used to your advantage.

27. I
NOURISHMENT, PROVISION

This is not a time for action. Take care of others and see that
they are well-fed and well looked after. Rest and build up
physical strength for times of action. If every part of an enterprise works together
in the right rhythm, much can be accomplished; otherwise losses will result.

28. Ta Kuo
GREAT EXCESS, WEIGHT, INNER STRENGTH

Even a heavy branch breaks when it is overloaded, so, like
the branch, you shouldn't take on too much at this time. In
business, this is a warning against too much expansion or working too hard.
This hexagram also advises caution to those who are thinking of taking up
with a younger lover or of rescuing one who has problems. If you need an
escape route, one will open up now.

29. K'an
WATER, A RAVINE, DANGER

Some Chinese rivers are huge, and they can be moody and
dangerous, so the Chinese treat water with caution. There
are pitfalls ahead and possibly even danger. Don't take risks and don't make
important decisions, but keep the lines of communication open. Guard against
theft, trickery, and misuse of alcohol. Women may have menstrual or other
reproductive issues.

30. Li
FIRE, CLARITY

Fire is seen as a source of light and knowledge, so
intellectual pursuits will go well, and an intellectual
approach will be helpful. Passion is likely to rule your head, and common
sense is advised whether this relates to a business decision or a matter of the
heart. This hexagram is favorable if your reading takes place in the summer,
unfavorable if in the autumn.

31. Hsien
ATTRACTION, RELATING

An attraction will bring people together, and this could
mean the start of a blissful love affair or a successful business
partnership. Avoid pressing others into doing what you want unless they
want it too. Don't envy those who appear to be more successful than you are;
remember, the bigger they are, the harder they fall.

32. Heng
DURATION, PERSEVERANCE, ENDURING

Stay put, persevere, and allow things to take their course.
Haste will bring problems. Don't insist on having things all
your own way.

33. Tun
RETREAT

Sometimes one has to step backward for a while. Business may
be poor, and you mustn't throw good money after bad. It is a
bad time to embark on a love relationship or get into anything new right now.
There are crafty people around you who will seek to take advantage of you, so
avoid traps. You may have to use some guile yourself in order to slide out of a
tricky situation.

34. Ta Chuang
GREAT POWER

If you have to use strong words, back them up with
meaningful action, or you will not be taken seriously. Take the
initiative and try to succeed, but don't be forceful when it isn't necessary. Treat
lovers gently and avoid throwing your weight around in the home.

35. Chin
PROGRESS, ADVANCEMENT

Your fortunes are improving. Be honest in all your dealings,
and be open so that jealous people will not be able to point
fingers. This is a good time for those in business or for career matters because
it suggests that promotion and success are on the way, but don't take an
aggressive stance.

36. Ming I
DARKENING OF THE LIGHT

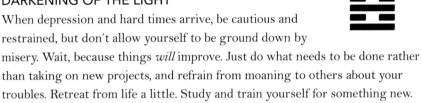

When depression and hard times arrive, be cautious and restrained, but don't allow yourself to be ground down by misery. Wait, because things *will* improve. Just do what needs to be done rather than taking on new projects, and refrain from moaning to others about your troubles. Retreat from life a little. Study and train yourself for something new. Keep secrets.

37. Chia Jen
THE FAMILY

Family life and domestic circumstances take precedence, and you need to cooperate with other family members. Attend to your normal daily duties; make your surroundings comfortable and your situation happier. Deal with problems immediately rather than ignoring them or trying to escape from them.

38. K'uei
OPPOSITION, CONTRADICTION

Be flexible and allow some leeway to others. Even if you *know* you are right, don't ram the fact down the throats of others. Expect opposition from colleagues at work and from family members in the near future. Keep quiet, keep your opinions to yourself, and try to fit in for a while.

39. Chien
OBSTRUCTION, DIFFICULTIES

This is a bad time for practically anything, and it is particularly difficult for love relationships. Don't moan, get help if you can, and wait for better times.

40. Hsieh
LIBERATION

An acute situation will come to a head, and at least now you will know where you stand. Free yourself from unnecessary encumbrances so that you are in a position to move forward. If you need a job, you will find it, and if something else is holding you back, it won't for long.

41. Sun
DECREASE

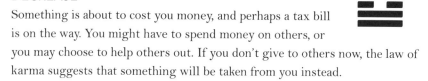

Something is about to cost you money, and perhaps a tax bill
is on the way. You might have to spend money on others, or
you may choose to help others out. If you don't give to others now, the law of
karma suggests that something will be taken from you instead.

42. I
BENEFIT, HARVEST, INCREASE

In times like these, even a total incompetent can succeed.
Business and finances are on the way up, and love or a loving
partnership could be on the way.

43. Kuai
DETERMINATION

The outlook for financial and career matters is good, but it
might be worth taking out insurance policies, and you should
avoid allowing bad behavior to destroy what you have achieved. Love affairs are
likely to be difficult, with quarrels spoiling the atmosphere.

44. Kou
ENCOUNTERING, TEMPTATION

This is a good time to flirt a little, to try dating a number of
different people, and to enjoy the social side of life, although
serious commitments don't seem to be in the air right now. Business matters
prosper, but in both business and social life you should avoid being influenced
by others. Calm persuasion will help you influence others.

45. Ts'ui
GATHERING, ASSEMBLING

Personal relationships should be happy, and there could be a
family celebration in the making. Work is okay as well. Don't
be difficult for the sake of it; just go along with the crowd and the general mood
around you for the time being.

46. Sheng
ASCENDING, ADVANCING

Don't give up; move steadily onward because progress can be made. Your efforts will be rewarded, and creative enterprises will be successful. You can bring bad luck upon yourself if you are arrogant, boastful, or unpleasant. Much the same goes for love and marriage because your own attitude and behavior will make love affairs succeed—or fail.

47. K'un
OPPRESSION, ADVERSITY

There will be hard times soon, so look within yourself for the strength to cope with them. Adversity can sometimes be character building, so have confidence and don't beat your head against the wall. Stay calm and cope as well as you can.

48. Ching
THE WELL

Work may be monotonous, but it has to be done. Share any benefits that you have accrued with others but see that they don't take the credit for your efforts or put difficulties in your way. If you have to choose between people or paths, use your intuition and avoid people who are dishonest.

49. Ko
REVOLUTION, CHANGE

The wheel of fortune is turning, and you may soon move to a new house or change your job. Getting together with a lover, splitting up with one, or even political changes are in the air. Your outer manner and presentation will improve, and you will impress others.

50. Ting
THE CAULDRON

Ancient people looked after their tools because they couldn't pop out to the store and replace them easily, so ensure that your tools, equipment, and vehicles are in working order. Don't worry about small mishaps but guard against larger ones. Eat well and cook something nice for those you love.

51. Chen
THUNDER, SHOCK, TURMOIL

There is stormy weather ahead, but don't panic. Just wait until it passes and then reassess your situation. Oddly enough, this is a good time for anyone who communicates for a living.

52. Ken
STILLNESS, KEEPING CALM

Take things easily and progress slowly along your present path. Don't take unnecessary gambles or take on more difficult jobs than those you are already coping with. Peace, love, and harmony can be expected at home.

53. Chien
GRADUAL DEVELOPMENT

Happiness will be assured in love or partnerships, as long as you keep to the rules and don't embark on an affair. In all other things, let matters develop slowly, even though there doesn't seem to be much progress at the moment.

54. Kuei Mei
THE MARRYING GIRL, THE MAIDEN

Harkening back to the time of arranged marriages, this hexagram counsels against getting into a situation that you can't get out of quickly, especially getting entangled in an affair. Avoid situations at work and elsewhere where you might be made into a victim. New relationships are not a good idea, but if you cannot get what you want, then at least want what you already have for the time being.

55. Feng
GREATNESS, PROSPERITY, ABUNDANCE

You will be inwardly happy, and troubles that come from outside will not harm you. Success, brilliance, and prosperity are indicated, but there is a warning not to overexpand or to overstep the mark. This is a good time to consolidate your gains, but not to lay out money on new ventures.

56. Lu
THE EXILE, TRAVEL

This is a good time to travel on business or pleasure! In short, you need to get away and see what the world has to offer. You must market yourself, possibly while looking for a new job, so improve your manner and your grooming regimen and be careful with whom you associate.

57. Sun
PENETRATION, PERSISTENCE, GENTLENESS

You must persevere with what you are doing, and if you are reasonable, others will accept your ideas. This is an excellent time for those who travel for business or pleasure or those who need to deal with people in other lands. Bend with the wind, and don't be argumentative.

58. Tui
JOY

This is a great time for career and financial matters, especially those that involve communication. Careers that rely on talking, singing, acting, teaching, or diplomacy will succeed now. Inner contentment will be reflected outwardly to others, and outer harmony will generate inner peace.

59. Huan
DISPERSION, REUNIFICATION

This may mean a move of house, a new venture, a change of job, a new car, or recovery from illness. This is a great time to alter your attitudes and brush up your appearance. A family may become scattered due to one or two relatives stretching their wings or moving on to improve their prospects. Marriage and relationships will be on the back burner for a while because you will be too busy traveling and working to concentrate on these matters.

60. Chieh
LIMITATION

You need to be cautious and to accept certain limitations. Reserves of energy, goods, or money will be needed while you sit out a difficult situation. You will move forward when the right time comes, but for now go by the rules—even if they are someone else's.

61. Chung Fu
INNER TRUTHFULNESS

Be true to yourself and sincere toward others, and you will gain their trust. This hexagram predicts improvements in your career, business, financial matters, and especially for matters of the heart. A move of house or a move across water is possible, and a change of scene will be beneficial. Some Chinese texts suggest that there will be stormy weather ahead, but this is probably due to the upheavals that change brings.

62. Ksiao Kuo
SLIGHT EXCESS, MODERATION

Your progress will be halted, which may be due to external forces or your own negativity or fear. Don't be a miser; give generously of your time and resources, and these will be repaid. Don't waste your energy or get into a panic, and if storms arrive, keep calm, stay safe, and wait for them to pass.

63. Chi Chi
COMPLETION

A cycle has ended. Consolidate what you have achieved thus far so that you can build for the future. You must guard against losing all you have gained through stupid actions. Marriage or a serious relationship are favorable at this time, possibly because the courtship phase has been completed.

64. Wei Chi
BEFORE COMPLETION

The previous hexagram is called Completion, and now we have one that is called Before Completion, which appears backward at first glance, but in practical terms, it suggests that you clear things up before you end the current phase. You might have a final exam to study for, stuff you need to throw out prior to a move, or something else to finish up. Whatever the situation, clear the clutter and wait, because something new will soon come your way.

Changing Lines

You may remember that I suggested earlier that you mark the lines when you throw three heads or three tails, because these are known as *changing lines*.

This example shows a hexagram with the top line and the second line from the bottom as changing lines.

Any continuous yang line that is marked with a cross should now be changed into a broken yin line and vice versa. This will give you a completely different hexagram to check out after the first. This gives you a deeper reading, but it also moves your reading into the future, showing how your situation is likely to develop over time, with advice, warnings, or comfort for the future.

Bringing the Magic of the I-Ching into Your Life

While it might be nice to own your own Chinese coins, it really is not necessary. You can begin with what you already have in your wallet. However, it is important to remember that whatever coins you use for this process are treated with respect. If they are simply tossed as a party trick, then the oracle will respond with an equally frivolous answer. When the hexagrams are given time and reverence, deep wisdom can be absorbed and used for further growth and practical use.

✳ ✳ ✳

14

DIVINATION
THROUGH
DICE

Dice divination, or astragyromancy, goes back as far as 5000 BCE. The first dice we know of come from the Middle East and were commonly made from the knucklebones of sheep and other animals. These bones, called *astragaloi* by the Greeks, are a rough cube shape and were the forerunners of the dice we use today.

Dice are easy and inexpensive to obtain in modern times, and there are many variations on the market. Dice with one hundred sides and more have been created, but for this book, I am concentrating on the common six-sided die. These are not difficult to get hold of, since they are included with many board games, but they can be bought on their own as well. It is essential for the divination practices described here that the dice you use are different colors or otherwise easy to tell apart.

Simple Questions

There are many methods of working with dice, and due to the numbers on each face, numerology can play a big part in interpretation. We will look into this angle a bit later, but the easiest way of obtaining an answer is to use just one die and have a set answer for each number. This simple way of working gives direct answers but will not delve deeply into a question or give meaningful guidance.

To begin with, you will need to formulate your question. Unlike with other kinds of divination, this is one style that responds well to direct questioning. You might want to ask something like, "Would now be a good time for me to change my career?" or "How likely is it that I will begin a relationship this year?" On a roll of a die, an answer is given. The interpretations for each might be as follows, but you can come up with your own as well.

⚀   The oracle suggests yes.

⚁   The oracle suggests no.

⚂   The oracle suggests that you wait, for the time is not right.

⚃   The oracle suggests that you direct your attention to other more pressing matters.

⚄   The oracle suggests that it is likely, but there will be conditions.

⚅   The oracle suggests that the matter is out of your hands.

Using Numerology in Dice Reading

More commonly, diviners use two dice so they have a greater range of interpretation open to them—one to nine instead of one to six. To begin, you need to consider a question. Unlike with the previous method, this time the questions will need to be open for guidance from the oracle. Rather than questions beginning with "Will I?" or "Should I?" you would do better to ask questions beginning with "How might I . . . ?" or "What might I need to do to . . . ?"

Once the dice have been thrown, add the two numbers together. You will then need to reduce the number to a single digit between 1 and 9. For instance, if you rolled 6 and 4, you would first add them together to make 10, and then further reduce them to make 1 (1 + 0). Alternatively, if you threw 6 and 6, you would add those together to make 12 and then further reduce them to 3 (1 + 2). The following interpretations are based on numerological significance.

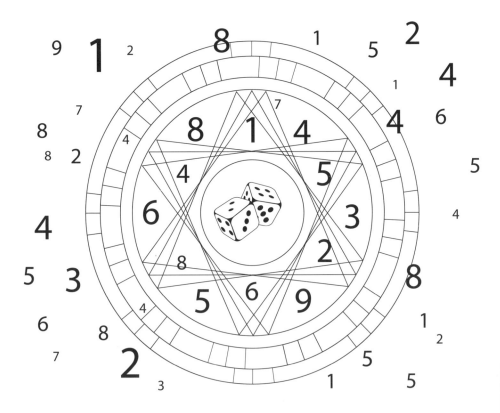

One

A new beginning is before you. Therefore, opportunities and fresh starts are noted, and you are being encouraged to consider all new possibilities. This could mean leaving previous situations, projects, or people behind, but this cannot be avoided. A new cycle is beginning.

Two

Now is a time to make a choice. Decisions are not always easy to make since they will often involve other people, and sacrifices may need to be made. Partnerships are important, so joining with someone new could be forthcoming.

Three

Now is a time to develop something and create your dreams. If you have a goal or your question concerns ways in which you may move forward, it is time to nurture your passions and find practical ways of manifesting them. Working with others could be part of this, since the number three often signifies a group.

Four

Security is yours at this time. If you have been concerned about the stability of a job or relationship, you are being advised that things will work out well. However, stability can sometimes leave people feeling stuck. You must ask yourself if building walls around yourself brings stability or creates a prison.

Five

Problems will arise, and you will be challenged. This is a difficult time, and struggles may become frequent with regard to your question. Do you

choose to fight against them, or would you do better to retreat and admit defeat? To accept that something is not working or that the time is not right is not a sign of weakness but, rather, a strength. It might save you much time, money, or emotional energy.

Six

Now promises to be a time of peace. You may have been through a difficult period, but harmony will soon be restored. This would be a good time to seek the advice and help of others, since support is available from those around you. Family and community are noted.

Seven

You may have a lot on your plate at this time, but you are being advised that you can cope with what is before you. Whereas a less-experienced person may crumble, you have the ability and resources to keep going and overcome tests. Challenges may prove difficult, but know that you have the strength to take them on and win.

Eight

You have gained wisdom and confidence. Those around you will notice your accomplishments and promotions of all kinds could be before you, as whatever you have invested time in is paying off. The outcome you have been considering may not have been reached just yet, but you are certainly on your way to achieving your goals.

Nine

An ending is nigh. In life, everything changes, and things must finish. While this might sound negative or even worrying, it needn't be. Everything has its shelf life, and from each ending will come something new and exciting. At this time, think about what no longer serves you and consider a clean break. Whereas some cycles end naturally, there are other ends that you must instigate for your own well-being and self-development.

Using the Dice Separately

There are a multitude of different ways to read dice, and some practitioners will use three or more dice for different methods. This is one reason that it is useful to include different colored dice within your practice, since different dice could stand for different areas of life if you wish. Blue may correspond to relationships, whereas red might represent romance, which when added to blue means romantic relationships.

With just two dice, it is possible to create a great number of interpretations. The following method uses the two numbers to reveal information around specific subjects.

As already described in the previous example, throw your two dice, and work out the value by adding the two numbers and reducing to a single digit. The following guide could help you to determine which area of life the oracle wants you to concentrate on:

1   Home and family
2   Work and career
3   Romance
4   Friendships and relationships
5   Creativity
6   Official events and activities
7   Spirituality
8   Recreation and leisure time
9   Money and finances

Now throw your two dice again. This time, rather than combining the values, note the numbers and find out where they intersect on the chart on the following page which will provide you with a word.

If you feel as though you need more input from the dice, you can repeat the second part of the process and add another word to the first. This will sharpen your interpretation.

1st Die

	1	2	3	4	5	6
1	Beginning	Conclusion	Abandonment	Movement	Delay	Ending
2	Partnership	Conflict	Reconciliation	Romance	Sexual Attraction	Agreement
3	Success	Failure	Victory	Justice	Friendship	Loneliness
4	Wisdom	Warning	Apathy	Advice	Change	Passion
5	Education	Healing	Support	Peace	Messages	Fear
6	Choice	Worries	Sadness	Loss	Deception	Reward

2nd Die

Here is an example of a dice reading using this method:

- Because the seeker did not have a question in mind, he started with part 1.
- After carefully throwing the dice onto a tray, the numbers 4 and 2 were revealed, suggesting *warning*.
- He then went on to throw the dice a second time and received 6 and 5. On the chart, the intersection of these two numbers is *fear*.
- To gain a little extra insight, he threw again and was presented with 2 and 3, suggesting *failure*.

The young man in this example said that he was buying a new home. He was fearful that it might not go through, since he was having trouble with the person buying his current home. Having already invested a lot of money, time, and emotional effort into the house-buying process, he was worried about how things would turn out, so the prospect of failure was a concern for him.

It is important to know which of the two dice you will read first and remain consistent. This is also why it helps to have two differently colored dice—so you can work with the same order throughout. When using a chart such as the one on the previous page, doing so is vital, since switching the numbers will provide you with a different word.

The words in the chart are just one example of what you can do, but you can easily create your own method. More than one chart can be created for the various throws.

Consider these alternatives for your dice readings:

Option One	Option Two
Initial throw—consult the chart	Follow-up throw—consult the chart again
Problems	Solutions
Situation	Context
Present	Future
Hopes	Fears
Conscious	Unconscious
Suggested action for you to take	What others may do
What to go toward	What to avoid

CONCLUSION

Divination is an art, and a practitioner can acquaint themselves with one or more methods. In some cases, different ways of divining can be combined. Some card readers enjoy fusing different systems, potentially pulling one tarot card after a Lenormand reading for a little extra insight or asking the questioner to draw a single rune as a way of inspiring action. This is when divining becomes individual to the diviner. Many of the practices described in this book will work effectively together, but it is up to the diviner to determine what works best for them.

I hope that this book has whet your appetite for divination and that it has given you enough information to get you started on your journey. Any book is just a beginning, and it could be just what you need to inspire you to become a successful diviner.

INDEX

IMAGE CREDITS

ABOUT THE AUTHOR

Steven Bright is a full-time tarot and oracle card reader who lives in Kent, United Kingdom. His first tarot deck, *Spirit within Tarot*, was published by Red Feather in 2017, and he is the author of *Tarot: Your Personal Guide*, *The Oracle Creator: The Modern Guide to Creating a Tarot or Oracle Deck*, all published by Liminal 11, and *The Gothic Oracle*, which was published by U.S. Games. He is also the cocreator of the *Rainbow Kipper* (Red Feather) and the cofounder/editor of *Esotoracle*, a magazine dedicated to divination of all kinds. In addition to speaking on the radio and giving public courses, Steven has presented at the UK Tarot Conference, the Tarot Association of the British Isles Conference, the London Tarot Festival, and for the World Divination Association.